FIRMLY PLANTED PUBLICATIONS
An imprint of Equipped for Life Ministries, Dallas, Texas

The Prodigal Paradigm

The Bible's Real Storyline

B. Dale Taliaferro

The Prodigal Paradigm
published by Firmly Planted Publications
an imprint of Equipped for Life Ministries

Copyright © 2015 by B. Dale Taliaferro
International Standard Book Number: 978-1-950072-04-0

Printed in the United States of America by
Morris Publishing
3212 East Highway 30
Kearney, NE 688847
1-800-650-7888

Scripture quotations take from the New American Standard Bible®, Copyright © 1960, 1962, 1963, 1968, 1971, 1972, 1973, 1975, 1977, 1995 by The Lockman Foundation (www.Lockman.org). Used by permission.

ALL RIGHTS RESERVED

No part of this publication may be reproduced, stored in a retrieval system, or transmitted, in any form or by any means, without prior written permission.

For information:
Equipped for Life Ministries
P.O. Box 12013
Dallas, Texas 75225
U.S.A.
www.e-l-m.org

Library of Congress Number:

Revised Edition / First Printing / 2019

WITH THANKS

I want to thank Carol Trebes for reading, editing, and making valuable suggestions to the manuscript. My wife, Waunee, I want to thank for taking care of the seemingly endless issues that must be done to make the manuscript ready for publication. Also special thanks goes to Maritza Ortiz who helped format the initial editions of the manuscript. I must also recognize Curtis Tucker who helped in condensing and popularizing the final edition, making the presentation flow better. In addition to these just mentioned, are those who have been used as God's "goads" in my life to make me review what I had been taught, to question, even to play the Devil's advocate against what might be termed mainline thinking, and to have the courage to change my views when God's Word seemed to require it. I know this has been a labor of love for which I am deeply grateful. Thank you all.

DEDICATION

I want to dedicate this book to all the people who have been frustrated in their study of God's Word because it didn't seem to say what so many were telling them it had to be saying. As these professional teachers and preachers expounded the Bible from preconceived theological notions, it became obvious that their interpretations either seemed forced at various points or assumed a lot of information that was not given in the passages being studied. My hope is that this book will encourage every reader to get back to his own personal Bible study because he can understand it on his own. It is a simple book overall, given by God for all of His people. I hope that you will all learn to cherish it as God intended you to do. May God bless His truth retold in this presentation and may His people become enamored once again with the God of all grace.

TABLE OF CONTENTS

Preface to the Revised Edition 9
Preface 11
Introduction 13

Chapter 1 The Big Picture 23
    The Existence of God, Assumed 24
    God's Adversary: … the Devil 30
    Humans Placed in the Middle 34
    Spiritual Death Explained 36
    The Purpose or Plan of God 39

Chapter 2 Adam and Eve 41

Chapter 3 Adam and Eve's Three Sons 47
    Cain, the Coming One? 47
    Abel, the Righteous One 54
    Seth, the Second Abel? 56

Chapter 4 Noah 59

Chapter 5 Abraham 63
    Abraham: the Original Heathen in Africa? ... 66
    The Sufficiency of Natural Revelation 71
    Abraham Believes in God, Becomes Useful ... 74
    Abraham's Walk was Justified by God 78

Chapter 6 Abraham to Moses 83
    Isaac Believes in God, Becomes a Useful Son .. 83
    Jacob Believes in God, Becomes a Useful Son . 87
    Joseph Believes in God, Becomes a Useful Son. 91
    Joseph's Brothers Believe in God, Become 93
    Moses raised up as Savior 99

    The Three Signs Given to Moses 100
    The Design of the 10 Plagues 103

Chapter 7 Israel: from the Exodus to the Exile 107

    The Wilderness Generations 108
    Israel: In the Land and United 111
    Israel: One Nation, Two Kingdoms 113

Chapter 8 The Testimony of Hebrews 11 119

Chapter 9 Jewish Belief at the Time of Christ 129

    Nicodemus, a Pharisee & The Teacher in Israel 131
    The Samaritan Woman at Jacob's Well 140
    The Nobleman & his Household 145
    The Healed Lame Man 149
    An Overview of the Rest of Jesus' Addressees 153

Chapter 10 The Unpardonable Sin 155

Chapter 11 Distinguishing Acceptance, Justification
          And Salvation 163

    Acceptance by God 163
    Justification by God 165
    Salvation by Jesus 167
    The Book of Romans 169

Chapter 12 The Kingdom: Promised in the OT,
          Offered in the NT 177

    Jesus Came to Rule on David's Throne 178
    Jesus Can't be Ruling today 179
    The Kingdom of Heaven is Not in Heaven ... 182
    The Kingdom of Heaven is Not Salvation 183
    The Kingdom Described in the OT 184
    Israel's Rejection Delayed the Kingdom 190

Preface to the Revised Edition

This series of books was written during my spiritual journey. As a result, I now find the need to go back through each volume and make some necessary corrections and updates. I really didn't understand how many preconceived ideas that I was working from and that were still hindering my comprehension of the real message of the Bible. I still needed to confront several issues and hold them under the microscope of God's Word. For the sake of simplicity, I will summarize those issues here:

1. I developed a better understanding of the historical situations of some very important passages which changed my thinking relative to their meaning. As a result, the unpardonable sin has been revised. Basically, the unpardonable sin is a rejection of Jesus as the Messiah by the first century Jewish people, resulting in a delay of their earthly kingdom promised to them by God in the OT, and to their missing their own entrance into that kingdom in their mortal bodies.
2. I finally was able to move past my theological prejudices concerning Acts 16:31 and Eph. 2:8-9 by understanding salvation and faith Biblically. As a result, I have found that the Bible does not describe a person as being saved from hell because the term salvation never refers to a deliverance from hell once-for-all or in any other way. Consequently, these two classic passages on salvation have nothing to do with a rescue from hell with a promise of heaven. Those ideas have been read into these passages without any substantiation.
3. Since no one was ever described as a "saved person" by *initially* trusting in Jesus, I am led to reframe from

doing that as well. I eventually realized that even the apostles were not described as "saved persons" upon their initially trust in Jesus. *Salvation is not a standing or status before God that guarantees a person a heavenly home and an escape from hell.* Nor is it a permanent, unchangeable condition that is reached by initially (and/or continually) trusting in Jesus. We can be saved from temptations and sins, but we can't be saved from hell and given heaven due to a simple, but genuine, trust in Jesus.

4. Finally, I realized that while there is no concept in the NT that can be likened to the traditional idea of a "saved person" in Christian teachings, there is a NT concept of a *salvation that is taking place presently*. As a result, it is biblical to describe people as "being saved" from temptations and sins but not as having been saved once for all from hell with a guarantee of heaven. Since the Bible doesn't do that, neither should we. It is easy to see how this reinforces the new understanding of Acts 16:30-31 and Eph. 2:8-9.

With these discoveries, I was able to reach a consistent concept of salvation with nothing but the Bible as my guide. The biggest correction that I have needed in these volumes is to distinguish between a *spiritual* salvation that is defined as an ongoing deliverance from temptations and sins from the traditional, but mistaken, idea of a *spiritual* salvation that supposedly takes place at the moment of initial faith in Jesus and that supposedly obtains a deliverance from hell. While the former is clearly Biblical; the latter is a creation by men alone.

PREFACE

The premise in this book is simple. The Bible is *about an extraordinarily gracious and loving heavenly Father who is seeking to win back His lost, prodigal sons and daughters so that they can fulfill their calling, and He can fulfill His plan for planet earth.*

The Bible is confusing because we have been taught the wrong grid or paradigm for understanding it. If you want the message of the Bible to make sense to you, you must allow it to say what it is trying to say and not make it say what men and women through the centuries have mistakenly thought it should say.[1] To mindlessly propagate the views that have come down to us is an effective way to establish error as truth.

In short, the story the Bible is trying to set before us, from *Genesis* through *Revelation*, can be reduced to the premise and principles found in Jesus' *Parable of the Prodigal Son* in Luke 15.

In the process of understanding the Bible through the grid of a heavenly Father seeking His earthly prodigal sons and daughters, you will discover important distinctions between the initial acceptance by God that man *supposedly needs*, his *supposed* once-for-all justification, and his salvation that is *supposed* to occur at the same time that justification occurs. All of these things *supposedly* result in a secured place in heaven. This study will reveal that many of the things we *suppose* happen don't really happen like we've *supposed*. What has made sense to us

---

[1] See Stephen Lewis' article, "Consensus Theology Taints Biblical Theology," in The Journal of the Grace Evangelical Society, Autumn, 2010, pp. 25-39.

theologically is simply not what the Bible actually teaches. We have been guilty of passing on error.

I have cut the present manuscript down from 290 pages to its present length in an attempt to make the message as simple and as clear as possible. The material that has now been omitted attempted to explain some of the basic ramifications of what is being proposed. While those ramifications are extremely important, I am convinced that laying the foundation as clearly and as simply as possible is better than trying to be complete. Consequently, there are five sequel volumes already planned to address many of the most important questions that this study will raise. More may be added as needed.

And, of course, there are many consequences of this new paradigm that I have not worked out myself. I hope that others will join me and work together in developing a truly Biblical theology that will direct and motivate all of us to walk more intimately with the Father and with His Son through the ministry of His Spirit. This work is not a polemic or an apologetic; it is a presentation of the Biblical facts that ought to enhance our grasp of the storyline of the Bible and enrich our daily walk with God.

INTRODUCTION

I am using the term *paradigm* to refer to a way of looking at things; it is the *template* that we ought to use to make sense out of the facts that confront us in the Bible. While it is inevitable that this paradigm will be viewed by some as "just another theological grid," and I suppose that in some ways it is, it may differ a bit from those which have preceded it. It is hoped that this paradigm lacks the rigidity of a too narrowly conceived plan that not only misses the full scope of the divine purpose for man and the earth that he inhabits, but also the central focus that the Scriptures themselves labor to delineate.

Think of a paradigm as a window in your house. When you look through it, you view the world closest to you. If that window is small, it won't give much information about how big that world is nor how many relationships exist in it. If it is tinted, it will literally "color" the things that come into your view. And if the glass has been poorly made, it will distort images that enter into your field of vision.

A paradigm is very much like that. The wrong one will distort everything we see. Deceived by those distortions, we will draw false conclusions from the facts being presented to us. The obvious truths that are seen clearly lead us to *suppose* that other connections are equally obvious. But these connections are now based upon the paradigm that we are using to view the original facts of Scripture. And since our paradigm for understanding the facts actually misconstrue them, we are wrong in thinking that they are as equally valid as the facts of Scriptures themselves. So, our paradigm, our enormous assumption about how all the facts fit together, leads us to believe that we see all things clearly. Now as that conviction establishes itself within us, we cease questioning our own convictions. At that point we have committed spiritual suicide. It takes almost the direct intervention of God to bring us back to life.

Consider the reading of this book an experiment. I want you to walk with me through the Bible, applying a new paradigm to all that we see. I believe you are going to find out that the Bible will come alive to you in a wonderful way. The reason that this new paradigm will be such an enhancement to your Bible study is that it is not a preconceived idea to which we will force the Bible to conform. Rather, it is the motif that the Bible itself suggests for understanding itself properly.

Since the premise of this book is that the message of the entire Bible is the *Parable of the Prodigal Son* constantly repeated in Biblical history, let's begin with a brief overview of the teaching of that parable. It is one of the most well-known and straightforward parables that we learned in our earliest days of Biblical literacy. Even so, there are assumptions related to this parable and conclusions made from those assumptions that have caused it to be handled very differently by various readers. If you use the wrong paradigm to understand the Bible, you will be looking through a windowpane that distorts almost everything that you see.

Many have looked into this parable and found in it an evangelistic message. For example, some have said that in this parable Jesus is explaining how the "unredeemed" world comes to faith in God. Others have said that this is a parable intended to portray Jesus as the object of belief. Still other interpreters have suggested that Jesus explained in His parable how repentance is a necessary element for being saved. And another sees Jesus demonstrating man's need to humbly recognize his own sinfulness before he can be saved from hell. These conclusions have been made by many sincere scholars and have been included in the construction of innumerable evangelistic tracts.

What is seen in the parable is determined by the paradigm placed over it to understand it. In all candor I suggest that most readers believe that Jesus' parable teaches whatever his own particular theology happens to be. What might we learn from this parable if it isn't an evangelistic story? Would that make any difference to how it might guide us in constructing our world-view? Oh, indeed, it would!

So we come to the point of asking, what exactly is the *Parable of the Prodigal Son* really teaching?

An overview of the parable

A man had two sons. The younger son did not want to wait until the death of his father to receive his inheritance; he wanted his father to give it to him right away. This son was interested in living in the here and now. Patience wasn't his virtue. The father agreed to give him his portion early, and soon afterward this son left home, went far away, and squandered all of his inheritance, living a life of debauchery. When he had wasted his entire inheritance, a severe famine forced him to work in a pigsty. Finally, his extreme hunger, his destitution, and present hopelessness led him to return home to his father, hoping for the opportunity to work for his father as a hired hand.

As he approached the house, still being a good distance from it though, his father saw him, felt compassion for him, ran to him, hugged him, and kissed him. Dismissing his son's proposal of working as a hired hand, he called out to his servants to bring out the best clothes, sandals, and jewelry to put on him. He then commanded his servants to roast a lamb for a party to celebrate his son's return. The reason given by the father for the celebration was that . . .

> "this son of mine was *dead*, and has come to *life* again; he was *lost*, and has been *found*." (Lk. 15:24, emphases mine)

The italicized words in this verse are the "red flag words" which cause so much confusion when people pour meanings into this parable that are not inherent in it. The window one uses to look into the parable will determine the meanings that the reader will see in these words. Those meanings originate in the theology of the interpreter rather than in the intent of Jesus who tells the story. This is the reverse of what should take place. But this is the unfailing result of looking through the wrong window into the Scriptures.

When the older son came in from working in the field and found preparations being made for a party for his younger brother's return, he became very angry. He would not participate in the party even after his father urged him to join in. He complained to his father, comparing his faithful service to his father (which had never been rewarded with a cook out with his friends) to his brother's licentious lifestyle that had wasted his father's wealth.

The father responded to the older son's complaints by asking him whether he (the elder son) had not always been with him (the father), implying that their relationship would have supplied everything he needed, even a party with his friends, if he had just asked for it. The father also explained to the older son that he was doing what any father would do who had another opportunity to be with his son whom he thought he might never see again. The party was a necessary expression of the love that he possessed for his son. He had continued to love him in his rebellion, but only now could that love be experienced by him.

The interpretation of the parable

The summary of the parable contains those same "red flag words" that tend to lead people astray in their interpretation if they are looking through the wrong window. Jesus' summary concluded with these facts:

> "But we had to be merry and rejoice, for this brother of yours was *dead* and has *begun to live*, and was *lost* and has been *found*."(Lk. 15:32)

Most, if not all, of the confusion in understanding this simple parable is due to the use of these red flag words that have grown in importance and significance by various commentators pouring into them the meanings that reflect their own theological understanding of the Bible. The tinted glass of their windowpanes forces them to color these words in a particular way. For them *dead* means having never been *alive*, and *lost* means having never been a son while *found* refers to saving faith in God. And so on. You get the idea I'm sure.

And sadly what is done to the parable is done to the whole Bible in exactly the same way! The window is the paradigm that we use to understand what we see. To the extent that it is poorly made we become confused if not completely blinded.

The amazing fact is that if one, simple truth is grasped in the parable, the overall teaching of it becomes almost self-evident. That one truth is this: ***the father had two sons***. These were not two young men who looked like the father's sons but who really weren't his sons. They weren't young men who acted like sons when they weren't his sons. They did not profess to be his sons when, in fact, they were pretenders. The father is their father … and they are his sons. This is an undeniable fact because Jesus, who told the parable, said,

"A certain man had two sons." (Lk. 15:11)

All the way through the parable, the father relates to both young men as his sons, and they relate to him as their father.[1] Nothing could be plainer. Furthermore, the fact that the father divides his wealth among them, designating to each son his inheritance, *forces* the reader to identify these young men as "sons" and as legitimate heirs of the man's estate.

They were true sons. There is no way around this fact.

But that fact didn't constrain either of the two sons to live a life of intimacy with the father that loved them so. Yes, *both* sons were missing something in their relationship, despite the fact that the emphasis seems to be upon the wayward son who returns.

Since these young men are already sons of the father, the parable couldn't have been given for any evangelistic purposes. That is the most important point to grasp as far as our present study is concerned. By misreading a text as *an evangelistic message* when in fact it is *a description of family matters*, the reader

---

[1] Lk. 15:12, 17, 18, 19, 20, 21, 22, 24, 27, 28, 29, 30, 31.

necessarily distorts the passage and creates lots of scenarios that were never meant to be taught in the first place. Confusion and theological chaos are the only sure results of such an error.

If the sons were *real sons*, then the intent of the parable was not to explain how the "unredeemed" world comes to faith in God. Its purpose is not to explain *the necessity of repenting* from personal sins in order to be *saved* in the traditional sense of that term. Its goal was not to demonstrate the need to *acknowledge one's own sinfulness* in order to be *saved* from hell. Neither was Jesus trying to explain how a person must come empty-handed before God in order to be saved.

The parable is simply not evangelistic in the slightest. It is not about the requirements needed to become a member of God's family. It is about sons, representing real family members, who were not experiencing intimacy with their father as he wanted them to do. The parable, then, is about God's desire for a loving relationship with His sons even when they don't love Him as they should. His love is abiding even though their love is like a vapor. His love remains steadfast even when they are living in sin.

Since this parable is about family relationships, a real son can be described as both *lost* and *dead*. When a son "walks according to the course of this world, according to the prince of the power of the air"[1] he is living a "dead (life) in his trespasses and sins."[2] To live a dead life is to be separated from the Father at any particular moment and in any particular area of one's life. Of course, as the youngest son illustrates for us, a person's whole life can be removed from any contact with the Father. The

---

[1] Eph. 2:2.
[2] Eph. 2:1.

wages of indwelling sin is always death![1] And death simply refers to a separation. In the case before us, it refers to a man's two sons who were separated from their father's incredible love.

A genuine son can be rebellious, lost, and dead, or he can be a hardworking, obedient son who is dead, having no vital relationship with the Father he is obeying. Both lifestyles portray the *living dead*; they are living because they are sons, but they are dead because they are separated from the father's love and grace. The Father, on the other hand, steadfastly loves them both as He waits for them to give the kind of response that allows them to experience His deep, deep love for them.

What every wayward son needs to do is to return home to his father for the meaningful life, with love, he always wanted.

What every self-righteous son needs to do is to realize that obedience must be performed by faith working through love.[2]

When a lost son returns home by repenting of his sins, or when he, if he has stayed at home in the physical sense, renews his love for his Father by repenting of his own lovelessness, it is a time for rejoicing! There is no thought given to the wasted time or wealth that has been incurred. There is too much joy over the reunion for that. The father's love removes all feelings of guilt.

This is the paradigm for understanding the whole Bible properly. This is the window through which the reader must view the message of the Bible for it to make sense to him consistently. This is the storyline of the Bible: the Father loves all of His sons and daughters, and seeks to restore the broken relationship that any may have incurred as he wandered from His presence and become lost in the process.

---

[1] Rom. 6:23.
[2] Gal. 5:6.

INTRODUCTION

If we equate the message of the Bible with the message of the *Parable of the Prodigal Son*, then *the storyline of the Bible concerns real sons, genuine sons, people who know and believe in the Father of heaven, but who often go astray and need to repent in order to restore their relationship with their heavenly Father once again.* The message of the Bible is not about the need for anyone to ***initially*** come to God in faith; rather, it describes what it takes to walk with the God that a person already knows exists and to whom he knows he is accountable.

I am sure you got that, but it is worth repeating nonetheless. The Bible's message is not evangelistic!

The Bible is about an extraordinarily gracious and loving Heavenly Father who is seeking to *win back His lost, prodigal sons and daughters so that they can fulfill their calling and He can fulfill His plan for planet earth.*

Lastly it must be noted that in Jesus' *Parable of the Prodigal Son,* there is no sufficiently "good son." Jesus' parable was given to portray the *religious leaders* and the *sinners* of His day.[1] The older son represents the religious leaders who stayed home, but who had no dependent walk with the Father while the prodigal son represented the outcasts of Jewish society who had gone astray from the God of their childhood faith and had wasted a good portion of their life in sinful living. But this latter group was now returning to the Father by responding to the Father's love that was being seen in Jesus. This was a love for all men around the world, but especially for those who lost their way.

Like the older son, the religious leaders worked for their heavenly Father without having a close relationship with Him. Like the younger son, the outcasts "came to their senses"

---
[1] Lk. 15:1-2.

through the ministry of Jesus and returned home to experience the grace and love of the Father whom they had taken for granted for some portion of their life. But their repentance and renewed appreciation of their Father's grace and love were not respected or trusted by the religious leaders who continued to see them only as "sinners."

There are good sons in the OT,[1] but they are few and far between as the old cliché goes. Most of God's sons, described in the OT for our instruction, represent one of the two sons in Jesus' parable. This is the reason that their ***initial faith*** in God or in a coming Messiah was ***never*** described. It is also the reason that their constant need was repentance, which is still best described as a "coming to their senses." Each time that they did, they returned to the love and care of their gracious God.

The whole Bible can be viewed without distortion if it is understood through this paradigm. Until we elevate the importance of God's children walking with Him to the place that the Bible has it, we've missed the central message of the Bible.

If we continue to try to understand the Bible from the theological paradigm handed down to us, we will continue to make the Bible about *other* people, people who are going to someplace really terrible unless they "get saved." In contrast, *the Bible is really about people who were created to walk with the God they know exists and to represent Him in all that they do.*

That is the paradigm that fits the whole Bible. It will certainly make us uncomfortable in places. But God knows that we all need to feel the heat before we do the right thing at times.

---

[1] The abbreviations OT and NT will be used throughout this book to denote the Old Testament and the New Testament, respectively.

So, let's test this paradigm together as we walk through the storyline of the whole Bible.

Chapter 1

The Big Picture

We have long been convinced that the message of the Bible is about getting to heaven and escaping a terrible place called hell. That message is set before us in this manner usually: God created this earth, and placed man upon it. Man failed and earned hell as a consequence of his sin. God sent Jesus to die for him. Then He raised Him from the grave so that He could save him from hell and get him to heaven. Now he has to live the best he can, holding on until he gets to heaven.

When you think about it, if that is the real message of the Bible, then it is a rather anti-climactic one. Nevertheless, it is the one that has dominated Christian thought, writing, and teaching for nearly fifteen-hundred years, going all the way back to the time of Augustine.

Did God really create this earth, make man, and place him on the earth so that after he sins, he could be saved, taken off this earth, and placed in heaven? Or do you think that maybe there is a whole lot more to God's plan for man and for planet earth than that?

From Genesis to Revelation God unfolds His plan, and He stays true to that plan without wavering from it until what He wanted in the beginning is seen in full blossom at the end. Only after He has accomplished His entire plan, do we read about eternity, portrayed, interestingly enough, as a new heaven and a new earth.[1] God's purposes for this creation must be fulfilled before "eternity" begins with "a new creation."

There is a recent book that every Christian ought to read. It is called *Majestic Destiny*. It was written by Curtis Tucker. In it, he answers the basic questions about life: why am I here, what am I supposed to be doing, and how will it all end? In other words, the book explains God's plan for human life upon the earth. He follows the development of God's stated intentions for man through the Bible from Genesis to Revelation. And he accomplishes his task in a very simple, easy-to-read manner.

So, he emphasizes the fact that the message of the Bible is not about heaven or hell; it is about God's majestic plans to establish His kingdom upon this earth and deal finally and fully with the rebellion of His adversary, the Devil.

As we begin our Biblical survey, we will let the Bible unfold naturally for us. Like the introduction in any book, the *Book of Genesis* explains for its reader the emphasis and plan that the author intends to develop in his literary work. When one surveys the first three chapters of Genesis, he is introduced to the main characters and to the direction that he can expect the rest of the story to travel.

Misunderstanding the plan, the plot, or the people leads to endless confusion which can hide the true message of the Bible!

The existence of God, assumed from the outset

The first person we meet in the introduction of the Bible is God. Now that seems like a fitting start, does it not? He is the originating cause of all creation. The only being that has life in Himself, as John 5:26 affirms for us, and not from another.

---

[1] Rev. 21:1—22:21.

If you begin with any presupposition, this is the safest and most reasonable of all: God exists. And the God that exists reveals Himself, His plan, and His purposes for planet earth.

While men have formulated philosophical arguments to establish a reasonable belief in God's existence, God reveals Himself by the things that He has made and by personally intervening into the affairs of men's lives. The first of these disclosures is called *natural revelation* because His self-disclosure is found throughout the natural creation that He has made. The second disclosure is called *special revelation* because His self-disclosure is contained in the specific communications He has had with man. All of the special revelation that a person needs to be fully equipped to fulfill all of his responsibilities before God has been written down and preserved in the Scriptures.[1]

But in the Old Testament eras, especially before the time of Moses and Job, God's revelation actually involved His personal intervention into the affairs of His creatures more than anything else. In fact, the whole OT is simply a record of God's intervention into the lives of mankind, both to individuals and to nations corporately.

The God who exists reveals Himself because He wants to be known. We must not think of the OT saint and what he had available to him in his day in twenty-first century terms. It was not until the time of Moses, generally speaking, that the Scriptures began to be written. And even then they were hardly available to every person. The common layman would never have had his own copy of the Scriptures that he could study for himself. He would have learned about God's special revelation either through oral tradition or through the teaching of the

---

[1] 2Tim. 3:16-17.

priests and prophets in the earliest days of the Jewish nation. Later he would have been taught God's special revelation from the Scribes and Pharisees after the establishment of the Great Synagogue around 444 B.C. These two groups, the Scribes and Pharisees, gave themselves to guarding and teaching God's revelation after it had been written down, compiled, and accepted by the Jewish people as their canon of Scripture.

The point that is being made here is that *the OT persons began trusting in God not from the systematic study of Scripture or as a result of philosophical arguments that led to the probability of God's existence. They believed in God because of their personal experiences with Him and through oral tradition.*

God had been faithful in making Himself known from the beginning of time. Consequently, the reader of Scripture repeatedly encounters individuals (outside of and unrelated to the nation that God had chosen to serve Him uniquely) who not only knew God but attempted to live their lives responsibly before Him.[1] How they knew so much about God had to come directly from God Himself.[2]

What you will discover as you read the OT is that God made Himself known through natural creation, in dreams and visions, and through theophanies (physical appearances of the pre-incarnate Christ), personal deliverances, and miraculous signs.

God revealed Himself to everyone in a variety of ways because He wanted a relationship with each of His creatures.

---

[1] E.g., Melchizedek in Gen. 14:17-20; Abimelech in Gen. 20:1-18. And if the passages in Exodus are related properly, namely, 7:5; 12:12; 14:4, we find that a whole nation appears to acknowledge the God of Israel as the Lord over all, even over their polytheism.

[2] The Book of Job is a wonderful study in this matter. Many believe that this book was the first written book of revelation from the God of the Bible. It contains an astonishing amount of revelation on the character and will of God. How did Job and his friends obtain this revelation? It is assumed here that he obtained it directly from God Himself.

God did not make it difficult or complex for His creatures to discover Him. He designed all people to seek Him,[1] and He is continually revealing Himself to them[2] as a motivation for their search.

It was not necessary for anyone, not Adam and Eve, not Cain and Abel, not Noah and his family, not Abraham, etc. to formulate philosophical arguments leading to a knowledge and belief in God. They all had firsthand experiences of Him. When an individual knows God personally, philosophical arguments for His existence become superfluous.

His intervention into the lives of the children of Israel was of such an extraordinary nature that the surrounding nations eventually heard of the miraculous deeds that He had performed, creating in them a fear of opposing such a God as watched over them. Consider Rahab's words to the spies of Israel when she was asking them to show mercy to her and her family:

> "I *know* that the Lord has given you the land, and that the terror of you has fallen on us, and that all the inhabitants of the land have melted away before you. For *we have heard how the Lord dried up the water of the Red Sea before you when you came out of Egypt*, and what you did to the two kings of the Amorites who were beyond the Jordan, to Sihon and Og, whom you utterly destroyed. And *when we heard it, our hearts melted and no courage remained* in any man any longer because of you; for *the Lord your God, He is God in heaven above and on earth beneath.*" (Josh. 2:8-11, emphases mine)

These are impressive words and unexpected convictions coming from a so-called pagan harlot. And we must not forget

---

[1] Acts. 17:22-29, esp. v. 27.
[2] Rom. 1:18-23.

that Rahab was speaking of events, one that was a miraculous crossing of the Red Sea forty years earlier and two others that were conquests of nearby kings that happened recently. One has to wonder about Rahab's spiritual condition at this point. And the spiritual condition of the whole city of Jericho should not be taken lightly either.

What would be your answer if I asked the question, *"Was Rahab **saved** (I'm using a familiar but inaccurate term) when her heart melted within her at the hearing of the miraculous provisions of Israel's God at the Red Sea?"* She knew that Israel's God was the God of heaven and earth, right? She even knew that He had given Israel the land of Canaan, of which Jericho was a part, right? That sounds like the kind of faith that Abraham had and that God reckoned for righteousness, doesn't it? It was.[1] In fact, Rahab's whole story has been included in the Scriptures to remember and honor these responses that she gave then.

In both Abraham's and Rahab's cases, God's reckoning of faith for righteousness was not at their initial faith in Him, but in their subsequent faith in Him. She had been a prodigal for some time; for how long we don't know. But she nicely fits into the category of "sinners" that Jesus described as the background for the *Parable of the Prodigal Son*.[2] And with the same love and compassion as He showed that son, He eventually drew her back to Himself by His providences and His revelations to her.

But we must not assume that, when God drew them to Himself, they were responding to Him for the first time. *In fact the Bible **never** describes a person's initial faith in Him.* Consequently, this reckoning has nothing to do with their

---
[1] Js. 2:25.
[2] Lk. 15:1-2.

inclusion into the family of God, with their being "saved," with their being forgiven, with their being given Christ's righteousness, or with their securing heaven as their eternal destiny. Such ideas present themselves because the reader is looking through the warped windowpane which has been given to him to understand the Scriptures. But it is not the interpreter's job to supply facts for the Bible or to connect its facts in ways that it does not *explicitly* do. I'll come back to this point when we investigate the classic passage on justification, Gen. 15:6. Not only does it describe Abraham's justification, but it also describes every other person's justification according to the apostle Paul.[1]

As far as Rahab's faith goes, there is no reason to suspect any deficiency in it from the information we glean from the Scripture. But since she was, like Adam and Eve, created to have fellowship with God, the proper assumption at this point would be that she was responding to the light that she had and found approval from God because of her proper responses.[2] And we must not forget that the Messiah comes from her physical line.[3] She not only believed in the one, true God, she also produced His Messiah!

At this point in OT history, Rahab portrayed a prodigal daughter who had returned to her heavenly Father!

The Bible is all about the Creator and Sustainer of all that exists and about how all that exists ought to give Him the praise due to Him. He reveals enough of Himself to every man to give that man a proper object for his faith. As John 3:16 tells us, God's

---

[1] Rom. 4:22-24.
[2] Heb. 11:31.
[3] Ruth 4:17; Matt. 1:5-6.

provisions extend as far as His love does, and His love is offered to all men.

God exists, and God speaks.

Why does God speak? Why does God reveal Himself?

He speaks to be heard. He speaks to be found!

He reveals Himself so that those who have strayed from Him may find their way back to Him. He speaks so that the prodigal sons and daughters will be motivated to return home!

God's adversary: the serpent of old, the Devil

Like any loving parent, God desires that his sons and daughters never wander away. He always wants the best for each of them, and His best always comes through an intimate, dependent relationship with Him. As we depend upon Him, He equips us to fulfill the calling for which He created us.

Yet there are other forces at work to seduce and draw all men away from their gracious and loving heavenly Father.

In chapter three of Genesis, God's adversary is introduced to the readers for the first time. At first he seems to be a talking snake. But that impression is tempered by other statements in God's Word that describe this same adversary by a variety of names. The apostle John, writing in Rev. 12:9 says,

> "And **the great dragon** was thrown down, **the serpent of old** who is called **the Devil** and **Satan**, who **deceives** the whole world ..." (emphases mine)

The *great dragon* refers to the angelic being instigating all the turmoil described by the apostle John in his apocalyptic book on the time of the unprecedented Tribulation coming upon all men living at the end of this present age. During that time in future history, this dragon will attempt to destroy the nation of Israel. The dragon's efforts will fail because God will intervene on Israel's behalf.

The *serpent of old* refers to God's adversary's first appearance before Adam and Eve in the Garden of Eden. He deceived Eve then, and he is continually trying to deceive the whole world up to this present hour.

The identity of the dragon and the serpent is then clearly given to us as *Satan* or the *Devil*. These two names refer to the same individual: God's great *adversary* (which is the meaning of the term Satan) who is adept in *slandering* (which is the meaning of the term Devil) God and His will. Every time God or His will is rejected the person doing it is essentially following the Devil.

This adversary is cunningly adept at enticing God's ambassadors away from their task of representing Him and at entrapping the prodigals so that they feel unable or too ashamed to return to their Father. But God is still in control of all things even if His control remains a mystery to us.

It should be noted that the serpent, or rather the individual who had indwelt the snake, was not allowed to come upon the scene to confront Adam and Eve until God permitted his entrance. Satan and God are not equals like the Ying and Yang in Chinese religious beliefs. They are not the necessary opposites that together bring a supposed balance to the universe. Satan was created by God since nothing that exists or has ever existed in original creation has come into existence in any other way than by the hand of God.[1] And as his Creator, God is Sovereign over him in every way.

In the *Book of Job* the reader discovers the true relationship

---

[1] John 1:3.

between God and Satan and the invisible battle between them over the hearts of the people God has created. When Satan came in before God, he was asked from where was he coming. Satan answered and said,

> "From roaming about on the earth and walking around on it." (Job 1:7)

Satan has been allowed great freedom by God even though, as Peter warns us in his first epistle, he is not to be taken lightly:

> "Be of sober [*spirit*], be on the alert. Your adversary, the Devil, prowls about like a roaring lion, seeking someone to devour." (1Pet. 5:8)

The Devil is on the prowl seeking to deceive and devour sons and daughters of the Father. He accomplishes his goal by using every means necessary to turn God's creatures away from fulfilling their divine commission of representing God as they walk with Him day by day. And if they are turned away from their divine calling, they must forfeit their future inheritance of ruling for God's Messiah in His glorious, earthly kingdom.

Satan's plan is to make prodigals!

God's plan is to show His grace and love to every prodigal, hopefully leading them all to repentance.[1]

That God is not afraid or worried about Satan's plans, his power, or his tactics is affirmed from the book of Job. God actually pointed out Job to Satan and asked,

> "Have you considered My servant Job? For there is no one like him on the earth, a blameless and upright man, fearing God and turning away from evil." (Job 1:8)

---

[1] Rom. 2:4; Cf., 2Pet. 3:1, 9.

And Satan countered God's appraisal of Job by suggesting that Job only served God because of what he got out of it. If God removed His protection from Job's life and took away all the blessings that had made his life so comfortable, and, in their stead, brought trial and turmoil into his life, then, Satan boasted,

"He will surely curse You to Your face." (Job 1:11)

Satan thought Job was an easy target to turn into a prodigal. If he accused you in the same way, would he be correct?

While Satan is correct in his analysis of all too many believers in God, as history clearly shows us, he was wrong about Job. So, God took the challenge and responded to Satan's accusations, saying,

"Behold, all that he has is in your power, only do not put forth your hand on him [physically]." (Job 1:12)

Satan has no authority or power to act independently. He must seek God's permission in all that he does. God tells Satan what He will allow him to do and exactly how far he can go in his endeavors. That ought to be incredibly encouraging. Every person can be assured that he is able to handle every trial or temptation that comes his way,[1] even if it comes directly from Satan himself,[2] if he, like Job, trusts God for everything he needs in everything that he does.

Satan, the great adversary of God and of godliness, has but one plan: to turn each person into a godless prodigal. Nevertheless, the rules of engagement are determined by God alone. Satan has no authority except what God grants to him.

---

[1] 1Cor. 10:13.
[2] Cf., both Js. 4:7 and Eph. 6:11-13.

So when Satan appeared in the Garden of Eden at the time he did, it was due to the fact that he couldn't come sooner because God would not permit his appearance until this time. And when he did come, he could only use the means that God had approved. It was in His power to form a hedge of protection around Adam and Eve just like He had done, by Satan's own admission, around Job who had lived after the time of Adam and Eve.

Satan had appeared at the beginning of the implementation of God's plan for man and for the planet he lives upon. From that point on, God has led in one direction while Satan has led in the other. God works to establish a mediatorial reign through humans upon the earth for His glory while Satan tries to oppose that reign to exalt himself.

Satan is a miserable glory-hound. And misery loves company!

Humans placed in the middle

Now we turn to man whom God created in His own image. Both male and female were created in the image and likeness of God. Hence, all humans were created to have fellowship with their Creator. But God also created mankind for a purpose, namely, *to represent Him and His will as he governed the world into which he had been placed.* As he exercised the dominion given to him over all that God had made,[1] he would live in a blessed state with the assurance of God's presence, leading, and care. God's purpose has always been to establish a kingdom in which man would "rule and subdue the earth"[2] on His behalf.

---

[1] Gen. 1:26, 28; Ps. 8:6.
[2] Gen. 1:28.

Unfortunately that purpose experienced some hiccups when Adam and Eve listened to the usurper about the forbidden fruit. And in doing so, they enabled him to become the "ruler of this world."[1]

But God's plan is a plan of restoration, victory, and dominion ... and it involves all men even after their personal fall into sin through their own choice. But the question that naturally arises in time is, "Does their sinfulness hinder their return to God or their subsequent rule for Him?"

Beginning with Adam and Eve, the *assumption* that the Bible presents to its readers is that the persons described in its storyline are just like the first couple after their fall into sin. They 1.) all know God as Creator and Sustainer even though most worship more than one god; 2.) they all know that they are responsible for walking with this God even though some suppress this truth more than others; 3.) they all sin to varying degrees; 4.) and they all experience God's temporal judgments upon their sinful ways. The spiritual dimensions of the main characters discussed in the storyline of the OT are more complex and not nearly as sanitized as we are commonly led to believe.

The people that follow Adam and Eve are never described as *eternally condemned* people on their way to hell. We have created that scenario. Furthermore, the Bible never tells us that man can escape hell only by believing in God or in His Messiah. We made that up too. *Rather, all of Adam and Eve's descendants remain people God created to have fellowship with Him as they represent Him while they live upon this earth.* But now they must do that, having something called *indwelling sin, a part of their nature* that must be mastered by each person separately.

---

[1] John 12:31; 14:30.

Indwelling sin lends itself to being victimized by Satan's strategies: it naturally leads us away from God,[1] and Satan provides the temptations that have been measured and calculated for each of our weaknesses to accomplish indwelling sin's natural tendencies.[2]

Spiritual death explained

Even after Adam and Eve's sin, the issue did not turn to the need to acquire heaven and escape hell. *Spiritual death* denoted a separation from God, but not the loss of one's ability to hear from Him, to understand what He requires, or to respond to Him in faith. *The ability to do all of these things remained, but the natural propensity to be with God or to draw near to Him had been lost.* Now man's natural inclination is to move away from God, rather than to move toward Him. Therefore, as we would expect, Adam and Eve hid from God in the garden. Once again, the apostle Paul called this sinful propensity ruling within all men *indwelling sin*.[3]

Spiritual death can be comprehended if we observe how spiritually dead people interact with God. First, that Adam and Eve died spiritually is garnered from the warning God gave them concerning their eating from the tree of the knowledge of good and evil. Eat of its fruit, God said, and you shall surely die. When they ate, they died.

Second, *spiritual death* did not impair their understanding or their ability to communicate with God. When God came looking for them, they interacted cogently with Him about their

---

[1] Js. 1:14-15.
[2] Eph. 6:11-12. Cf., also 1Cor. 10:13; 2Cor. 11:3, 13-15.
[3] Rom. 6:15-23; 7:13-25.

circumstances. They knew they had disobeyed God, but they tried to construct a reasonable excuse for their disobedience. This in essence is what indwelling sin does: it provides excuses for not doing what God wants done. It also provides the power to carry out the disobedience. And once it is in control, it can enslave the person in that separation from God, convincing him that he is not able to escape his spiritual dilemma. Indwelling sin convinces the person that the best he can do is what he is doing: trying to return but failing over and over. Its deception is basically this: spiritual victory is no longer possible.[1]

Adam said that their transgression wasn't his fault. He suggested that it was Eve's fault, the woman that *God* had given to him. Well, that was pretty good reasoning since Eve was the first to eat the fruit before she gave it to Adam afterwards.[2]

Then Eve said that it really wasn't her fault since she had been deceived by the serpent that *God* had created and allowed to be present in the garden. That was also pretty good reasoning since her transgression was not an action of rebellion, but the result of having been deceived[3] by an adversary that God allowed to confront her.

But God made it clear that all three, Adam, Eve, and the serpent, were culpable. *The act was wrong regardless of the reason supporting its performance.* We should observe that Adam and Eve didn't argue with God's evaluation of their situation or with the consequences He placed upon them.

...

---

[1] Rom. 7:11, 25.
[2] Gen. 3:6.
[3] 1 Tim. 2:13-14.

THE PRODIGAL PARADIGM

> *Their rationalizations ended at the moment God spoke to them.*
> God can, and does, communicate clearly and effectively
> with the most biased person living in sin.
>
> ...

Though Adam and Eve were spiritually dead, they still could be taught and convicted by God; they could receive what He was saying to them; *they could respond in a way that would heal the broken fellowship that they had experienced with Him.* That Adam and Eve did actually respond properly was, apparently, what happened. The story continues with Adam and Eve now in possession of indwelling sin, but still having the privilege of communing with God in a similar fashion as they had up to the moment of their first sin.

God was not through with man, despite his sin, because he is central to the big picture of what God has planned for this earth.

Third, one ought to observe what is missing in this passage if our traditional understanding of it were correct. There was no attempt to get Adam and Eve to admit their sinfulness, to repent of their sin, to trust in God to *save* them (from the eternal condemnation of hell, which is the traditional sense of the term *save*), and to commit themselves to a life of holiness. In short, a traditional gospel message, one that was intended to *save* Adam and Eve from hell, was not offered. *There was no evangelism attempted by God* toward the fallen, first couple.

Adam and Eve had sinned and were at a crossroads. If they continued to live independently, they would become prodigals. Their need was the same, nevertheless, as that of any prodigal: they needed to repent, to come to their senses, and return to their relationship with the God of all grace who abounds in lovingkindness. But this repentance was never for the purpose of escaping hell. It was for the purpose of returning to fellowship with their God.

A son is a son whether he is at home or far away. But a son may be a prodigal at home as well as far away. What makes a son *useful* to his heavenly Father? A trust in Him to supply all that is needed for him to represent Him well is his need.

The purpose or plan of God

As we allow Genesis chapters one through three to set the stage for the message of the entire Bible, we naturally conclude that the purpose of God is *earth-centered*. Heaven is not mentioned as a final destination or even as a goal to be sought. Nor is it an end to be obtained later through some means yet to be revealed. *As far as the story goes, the location of all the significant action that is anticipated in this introduction is the earth.*

This fact is essential for grasping the big picture of the Bible.

In like manner, hell is not set before the reader as a possible destination if man is bad or disobedient. The punishment that God warned Adam and Eve about was *spiritual death*, but this death occurred immediately, and was not a reference to some judgment in the after-life. *The story is about this earth and God's plan for man to rule upon it.* That is what the introduction of the Book of Genesis, the first chapter, so to speak, of the Bible, tells us.

As in Jesus' *Parable of the Prodigal Son*, we find that God's "sons" constantly turn away from Him. And just like in Jesus' parable, all of God's sons and daughters have issues, but He hopes that His abiding love for them will lead them to spiritual purity and maturity eventually. Each one is responsible for carrying out the commission for which God had created him: *to represent Him in his rule over the earth as he maintained fellowship with the God who had created him.*

As in the *Parable of the Prodigal Son*, our Heavenly Father is standing and looking for His sons and daughters who have gone astray to return to Him. One can go astray in "the far country"[1] or in "the household of God."[2] He can go astray as a *sinner*[3] trapped in a disobedient lifestyle or as an obedient son[4] who works for his Father without experiencing the intimacy that ought to accompany his obedience.

And we are taught to judge people by what they do, right? But when we look only on the outward appearance, because our ability ends there, we conclude that the former is in sin but not the latter. How wrong we are!

God sees the heart as thoroughly as He sees the hand. And for both of these sons, God has a plan for their lives ... and it is a good plan.[5] When He sees them from a distance, returning to Him, or when He hears them come in from the fields of labor, seeking Him, He will have compassion on them, run to them, embrace them, and kiss them.[6]

When they return, it will be a time to celebrate!

That is the big picture.

That is the storyline of the Bible.

That is the Prodigal Paradigm!

---

[1] Lk. 15:13.
[2] Cf., Matt. 21:32; 1Tim. 3:14-15.
[3] Lk. 15:1-2.
[4] Lk. 15:29-31.
[5] Jer. 29:11.
[6] Lk. 15:20.

Chapter 2

Adam and Eve

When we jump into *Genesis* two and three, we find man and woman as God had first created them. At the end of the six days of creation Moses recorded God's descriptive evaluation of all that He had made:

> "And God saw *all* that He had made, and behold, it *was very good*." (Gen. 1:31, emphases mine)

To declare that Adam and Eve were *good* means that they functioned exactly as God had created them to function. Being good had no connotation of morality. This is the reason that the mountains, the sun, moon and stars, the rivers and oceans, the trees and shrubs can all be called *good*. They functioned exactly as their Creator had intended them to function. Being good, Adam and Eve were naturally dependent upon God seeking to glorify Him in all that they did.

Furthermore, being good in this context meant that they were righteous both in who they were and in what they did. They came into the world with a constitution that naturally led them to experience a right relationship with God. There was no other inclination in them. There was no other life known to them. This seems to be required by God's pronouncement that their created condition was *very good*.

In his book entitled *The Existence and the Attributes of God*, Stephen Charnock suggested almost three and one half centuries ago that the term *good* was not being used as the opposite of wicked or sinful. Rather, it denoted the beneficence, bounty, and natural perfection of a thing created by God.[1] The immediate context demands this perspective. So, the term *good* referred to the fact that God created everything to function in a certain way, and it all, speaking of the entire creation including the man and the woman, functioned exactly as He had designed it to function. There were no slip-ups; there were no design flaws. Everything was right or righteous in every aspect.

Adam and Eve were created to know God, to love God, to obey God, and to worship Him, having fellowship with Him at all times. Every response they gave was in faith, pleasing to God naturally. But they were not an exception to the perfect functioning of the rest of creation. Adam and Eve didn't know what it meant to be a prodigal!

...

All of Adam and Eve's descendants are left to obtain by faith the intimate relationship with God that their original parents had by creation.

...

Most of us are taught to think not in terms of a relationship with God as a heavenly Father but in terms of a legal standing before God the righteous Judge. Consequently, we become *sons* and *daughters* when we are legally acquitted of the guilt and penalty resulting from our sins and sinfulness. Typically, we are taught that this legally acquitted status has **never** been obtained

---

[1] Stephen Charnock, *Discourses upon the Existence and Attributes of God*, 2 volumes, Baker Book House, Grand Rapids, Michigan, reprinted in 1979 from the 1853 edition by Robert Carter & Brothers, 2:217, 218-19.

through good works; it has always been gained by grace alone (or possibly by grace through faith).

But the concept of being legally acquitted is not present in the opening chapters of Genesis. And by the end of our study, I hope to demonstrate that such an idea is not to be found anywhere else in the Scriptures when either salvation or justification is being discussed.

The Bible never, absolutely never, deals with the moment a person *initially* places his faith in God. It is at that point, we have been taught, that a person receives his legal acquittal. But if that point is never dealt with by the authors of the Bible, that legal paradigm must be seen as a hindrance to understanding the message of the Bible rather than a guide to it.

Cain's, Abel's, and Seth's faith in God can be deduced from the text as I will show in the next chapter. Hardly anyone would even begin to question Noah's faith. And in Abraham, who came along over two millennia after Adam and Eve, we have the first explicit example of *a man maintaining fellowship with God through faith*.

In every case, we are led by the Scriptures themselves past any comment on or description of an anticipated, initial faith in God. That event, which seems to be so important within theological circles, is not a critical matter to the authors of Scripture since they all omit any reference to it. We must demand an answer to the question, "Why is there no reference to this?"

Adam and Eve walked with a *theophany* in the garden. Their experience describes an uninhibited fellowship with God of the most intimate kind since there was nothing to hinder it from being all that it was designed to be in God's *good purposes*. This theophany is presumed to be an appearing of the pre-incarnate Word[1] who would eventually take on the form of a bondservant permanently and become the promised Messiah. Jesus plainly told us that no one has ever seen God the Father;[2] but this one, the One appearing in the Garden, and later on various other occasions, was seen. Therefore, it could not be the Father; it must be a pre-incarnate revelation of the Father's Son[3] that was seen.

Walking with God in the garden, talking with God in the garden, responding to the commands of God (to name the animals, e.g.,) in the garden with obedience, and seeing a theophany that claimed to be God, the Creator and Sustainer of everything one could see or touch (and the Person to whom one was accountable), all of this describe the highest expression of fellowship one can have, don't you think? What more could be imagined than what they were experiencing? Wouldn't you love to have to *settle for* these same experiences today?

Adam and Eve's spiritual condition

If we take Adam and Eve's experiences at face value, doesn't it appear that they were individuals who had a wonderful walk with God? But Adam and Eve were set in the Garden of Eden for a test. What exactly did God's test concern? What was its purpose?

...

Adam and Eve's test had only temporal consequences.

...

---

[1] John 1:1-3, 14.
[2] John 1:18.
[3] Cf., Prov. 30:4.

Many assume that their test related to their eternal destiny. But there is not the slightest hint of such a view in the context. *Their trial was related to their **ruling for God** in the environment that He had placed them; it wasn't related to their supposed need of eternal salvation.* The issue wasn't about going to heaven and missing hell; the issue was about serving as God's appointed rulers by carrying out God's expressed will.

Their walk of faith, as they represented the God who had created and commissioned them, would have come naturally for them. Because they were created good, they functioned in complete dependence upon God. They would not have known what it was like to be independent from their Creator, living a prodigal lifestyle as a desirable alternative.

Another clear indication that Adam and Eve were already related to God is the fact that no one can die who had not previously been alive. When God warned Adam and Eve about dying if they ate from the tree of knowledge of good and evil, He was telling us indirectly, but plainly nonetheless, that at that moment they were alive spiritually. They had been created good, and a good creation is one that functions as it was intended to function as it came from the hand of the Creator. Adam and Eve, therefore, were responding perfectly to the opportunity to believe in and have fellowship with their Creator as they carried out His commands. They were at home with the Father and felt His love and experienced His care from day one.

Their sin caused a separation from God experientially ... but not eternally. After their sin, God's love and care and spiritual life itself could not be experienced naturally (i.e., as an automatic result of their creation). It was no longer their entitlement by creation. The more consistent they lived by faith from this point on, the more of God's love and care they would experience. What had been a natural experience for them became available to them only through *the choices of a persuaded heart* that God's will was best for them.

To belabor this a bit, let me say again that spiritual life, seen in the OT as *a spiritual connection to God*, would now be experienced only as a result of a faith response in God. But that would not be the only choice springing up within them. Now they would have two obstacles to overcome that they didn't have before they sinned. The first obstacle would be whether they would be guided by God's interpretation of the facts that confront them in life. Following God's guidance before they sinned was natural to them; they knew of nothing else. But now that response would be opposed at every step they took. It would be opposed by the change in their natures that had occurred when they sinned. Present within them now is an entity called *indwelling sin* which opposes God and His will.

That leads us to the second obstacle that of overcoming the lure of the lies, deception, and misinformation that would be springing from the Devil. He is adept at tempting each person in the areas of his greatest needs or weaknesses. He will question God's character and will at every turn.

What was once theirs naturally by creation must now come from a persuaded mind that is implemented in faith step by step. While Adam and Eve could have become prodigals, they remained faithful in their walk with God even though they now possessed indwelling sin. The roots of prodigality lay within their hearts, but they restrained those roots from manifesting their fruits by walking in dependence upon God.

Even though Adam and Eve had the privilege of walking in the presence of a theophany, they still had to walk by faith. They had to believe what this One, walking in their midst, explained life as it really is. While this was their natural response from their creation to their first sin, it would no longer be natural. It would be opposed from the outside and from the inside. But because of God's great love for them, He applied the work of the cross to them so that they had the capacity to continue their fellowship with Him and represent Him in all that they did. The cross, then, prevents total depravity from being man's default condition when he comes into the world even if indwelling sin were hereditary.

Chapter 3

Adam and Eve's Three Sons

The Paradigm of the Prodigal Son greatly helps us to understand Adam and Eve's descendants and identify all three of them as "sons." As the father in the *Parable of the Prodigal Son* had two sons, Adam and Eve had three sons. We need to understand that this is basically the opposite approach that we have learned in the past. And further, when we focus upon the three children of Adam and Eve, we are not suggesting that they only had three children. We are only observing that the three that are specifically singled out were meant to teach us about faith, family, and the impact those may have upon society and vice versa. It is clear from Scripture that Adam and Eve had other children.[1]

Cain, the coming one?

Cain was the first-born child of the first couple. Eve initially thought that Cain might be the fulfillment of the prophecy of the coming Messiah.[2] But she was later disappointed to find out that instead of being the promised conqueror of Satan, he would have trouble conquering the sin that indwelt his own heart.[3] And how much exactly did Adam and Eve understand

---

[1] Gen. 5:4.
[2] Gen. 4:1. If the italicized words in our English translations were all removed, Eve's initial response is much clearer: "I have gotten a man-child, the Lord."
[3] Gen. 4:7.

concerning the Promised One's bruising (or crushing) of the serpent's head? We don't know. The text does not give us that information. So, every interpretation of that verse is nothing more than human conjecture since the Bible doesn't interpret it for us.

By the time Cain is introduced to the reader, he is an adult and *is assumed to be a person who is responding to the God he believes in.*[1] Since the OT *never* mentions any person's initial faith in God, we ought not expect to find Cain's here. Therefore, the absence of it is no sign that Cain was a *lost, unsaved, eternally condemned unbeliever* (yes, I'm using terms that are familiar to us although they are all used inaccurately here).

Why does the OT never refer to a person's initial faith? The answer is quite simple. Initial faith is absent from the pages of Scripture because Cain and the other main characters in the storyline of the Bible are *assumed* to be already responding to God albeit inconsistently.

This *assumption* by the Bible about Cain is verified by several facts. First, we find him involved in worshipping the God who had walked with his mother and father in the garden. There was no opposing peer pressure coming from other humans outside his family. There was no reason to reject the training that Adam and Eve would have given to him. He would have been thoroughly educated by his parents about Satan and his methods to contradict God's will that was being given to them.

Also, this Creator God was, apparently, still walking among them. God did not leave the first family after the parents sinned in eating the forbidden fruit. Rather, He continued to manifest His presence to the whole family in some meaningful, but

---

[1] Cf., Heb. 11:6 for the probable content of his faith.

undisclosed way as we will discover in a moment. Consequently, Cain did not learn about the Creator God from the parental instructions given to him alone; he learned about the one, true God by personally walking in His physical presence just as his mother and father had done before his birth.

A second reason for assuming that Cain was a so-called *believer* is how familiarly God communicated with him after expressing no regard for his sacrifice. While the family is no longer in the garden, the Lord, apparently, still communed with all of them in a very similar fashion just as He had done when Adam and Eve were living in Eden. It is simply incredulous that such a walk could have no effect upon a person at all. Meeting with God face to face, or even in dreams and visions, if you like, had to impact him spiritually. It wasn't until Cain moved away after killing Abel that the text says that he "went out from the presence of the Lord."[1]

Cain became a prodigal son ... but he was not always one.

Moses used the phrase, "from the presence of," nine times in the Pentateuch; five of which are in *Genesis*. The phrase always referred to someone or something leaving a person's actual presence. Four times the reference is to the Lord's actual presence in some form.[2] In the other instances it refers to leaving Abraham's wife's presence,[3] or leaving Isaac's presence,[4] or leaving Pharaoh's presence.[5] In every case the presence from which something or someone is removed is a visible form[6] even

---

[1] Gen. 4:16.
[2] Gen. 3:8; 4:16; Lev. 10:2; Num. 17:9.
[3] Gen. 16:8.
[4] Gen. 27:30.
[5] Gen. 41:46; Ex. 2:15.
[6] Lev. 10:2 is a possible exception, but no one debates that the Lord had a real, localized

though it may have been hidden in a cloud. So when Cain left the presence of the Lord, he removed himself from some physical manifestation of the Lord who had walked with the first family all of his life up to that point. Cain, like the younger son in the *Parable of the Prodigal Son*, went to "a distant country" away from the presence of the Father.

...

The OT does not support the believer-unbeliever paradigm that we use so often today.

...

Third, the *assumption* of a vital faith within Cain is based upon the fact that God commanded him to subdue or to conquer his own indwelling sin. That would not be a command God would give to a person who was not responding in faith because it is not possible for anyone to carry it out except the person who was/is/could be walking by faith. Only such a walk frees one experientially from sin's natural tyranny and taint.[1]

In short, *Cain is presented to us as a person with a vital faith.* That should be the notion that the reader works with until he is *forced* to think otherwise. We must not let men's theological arguments mislead us. We ought to carry this notion with us as we study every reference to Cain in God's Word.

The Bible is not concerned about the moment Cain *initially* came to faith so neither should we be. What is important is that the Bible presents Cain as a person who worshipped the God he believed in even though at times he didn't worship Him in faith. Are we really any different?

---

presence in the holy of holies to which this is a reference.
[1] Rom. 6:6-23. For further explanations on this topic see my forthcoming book which explains chapter six of Romans in some detail.

Although Cain, indeed, murdered his brother Abel, that murderous act does not suggest that he was a so-called *unbeliever* (to again use our contemporary terminology which the OT does not support) any more than it suggests that King David was an unbeliever when he murdered Uriah[1] or that John Calvin was an unbeliever when he conspired to have Michael Servetus executed. There is no sin a believer is unable to commit, and there is no limit to the number of times he may commit it. Becoming unfaithful does not change God's steadfast commitment toward a person as Paul told us in 2Tim. 2:13:

"If we are faithless, He remains faithful; for He cannot deny Himself."

It is true that Cain is described in the New Testament as being "of the evil one."[2] And it is also true that the phrase "of the evil one" appears to be synonymous to "of the Devil," and to "son of the Devil," and to "son of your father the Devil." But that doesn't mean that these phrases refer to persons who weren't created and called to serve the one true God. Nor does it mean that these phrases can refer only to persons who never believed in God.

...

A person is "of the Devil" any time he is opposing God's will.

...

All the phrases, including "a son of the Devil" (or a son of your father the Devil), focus only upon a person's walk just as the phrase "son of God" does.[3] These phrases do not identify a

---

[1] 2Sam. 11:15.
[2] 1John 3:12. In context see 1John 3:5-11. Also cf., Lk. 9:55; Acts 5:3; John 13:27. See my book establishing the saved condition of Judas, entitled *Judas and Divine Grace*. Many are afraid of the Biblical doctrine of grace because grace can, in fact, be abused.

person as an "unbeliever" because neither the OT nor the NT supports the category as we use it today.

Such a handling of these phrases tells us more about the window that the interpreter is looking through to understand the Bible than it does about the phrases themselves. When the wrong window is used, a wrong paradigm is seen. This paradigm reveals the interpreter's theology but not what the Bible is actually teaching.

...

The OT contrasts the *righteous* from the *unrighteous*,
but never a "believer" from an "unbeliever."

...

We have foisted the believer-unbeliever paradigm upon the Bible. But it describes only persons who are walking in a way that pleases God or those who refuse to walk that way. It does not describe two identifiable groups, one of good people guaranteed of heaven and the other of bad people guaranteed of hell.

When we use the saying, "you little devil," we refer to the mischievous nature of the person being referred to more than anything else, right? The same is true of these phrases in the Bible.

It seems clear that Cain didn't persevere in his faith since he went out from the presence of the Lord and dwelt in the land of Nod (a name that means wandering). Because none of his descendants was described as a person who walked with God, many commentators describe Cain's line as *the ungodly line* while they denote Seth's line as *the godly line*. Seth's descendants are clearly said to have "called upon the name of the Lord."[1]

---

[3] Matt. 5:43-48, esp. v. 45; Rom. 8:14. Cf., Gal. 4:1-7 also.

The godly-ungodly rubric can be misleading because all too often it is used to connote that one line has all believing persons while the other line has all unbelieving persons. But this analysis is not feasible if for no other reason than the fact that Cain, the head of the ungodly line, was a person who exercised a vital faith in God for a while.

Because of Cain's dialogues with God in Genesis chapter four, it seems apparent that he had to have believed in God while, at the same time, he didn't want to obey Him wholeheartedly. (How can a person talk with God and yet not believe that He existed?) Cain became the first example of a person who worshipped God but not from the heart;[1] he was a man who, at least in one instance, went through the outward motions of worship but expressed no faith in it.[2]

...

Cain had to choose, and he chose death's independence over life's dependence.

...

Neither walking in the physical presence of a theophany nor having Him clearly set out His requirements for one's life inevitably leads to a spiritual response by any person. The heart of man after his first sin does not choose the greatest good that is such essentially; it chooses the greatest good as it perceives it in relation to itself. So when Cain made his choice, he chose the path of the prodigal for that path seemed best to him![3]

---

[1] Gen. 4:26.
[1] Cf., Isa. 29:13, a passage Jesus quoted to describe the religious leaders in the first century (Matt. 15:8-9).
[2] Heb. 11:4. And "without faith it is impossible to please God" (Heb. 11:2, 6).
[3] Cf., Prov. 14:12.

Apparently God made an indelible impression on all the members of the first family. He walked with them in some way for centuries. *He treated them all as His children.* Never once, as far as we know from the text of Scripture, did He offer a message or *a challenge to anyone to begin to believe in Him* as his Creator and the One to whom he was accountable.

That simply is not the paradigm the Bible sets forth.

Even further from the truth is the common *assumption* that Seth's descendants had to believe in a coming Messiah for them to be accepted by God. Since the text gives us no evidence that they had such a faith, we are reading into the text to surmise that they did. The need for a Messiah isn't even recognizable at this point in the storyline. Only by rearranging the Bible can the storyline be altered enough to discern the need for a Prophet-Priest-King Messiah.

The Bible simply presents Cain and his descendants to its readers as family members who were responding to the one, true God, but were doing so in varying degrees of faithfulness. The succeeding generations, apparently, believed in the God who walked before them, but these generations went astray, either manifesting Cain's example in his early life, when he tried to turn worship into a ritual, or his example in his later life when he finally took his family and went to the "far country," just as the prodigal son did in Jesus' parable. Hence, Cain represented both of the sons in the *Parable of the Prodigal Son* at different times in his life.

Abel, the righteous one!

Abel is a lot like Abraham's son, Isaac, in that he was a transitional figure. His life had meaning, but that meaning wasn't dependent upon his personal accomplishments. Rather, his meaning was dependent upon God's use of him in the lives of others.

...

Abel was a righteous man who worshipped God in faith.

...

Abel demonstrated for us what a life of faith looked like in the early years of man's existence. Much of what he knew about God was, presumably, taught to him by his parents and by God Himself who continued to commune personally with this growing family after Adam and Eve left the Garden of Eden and began raising their children. Abel's faith in God and his responsiveness to God's instructions to him were divinely approved[1] and rewarded by God.[2] As a result, he became an example for all who lived after him of one who walked by faith. This is the reason that he is included in the eleventh chapter of the Book of Hebrews, a chapter widely identified as *the hall of fame of faith*.

It was God's approval of Abel's life and specifically of his offering, while his own offering was shown no regard, that occasioned Cain's anger toward Abel.[3] His anger boiled until it led him to murder his brother. All men, but especially the Jewish people, ought to have learned from Cain's experience that the command not to murder included the idea of not allowing anger to dominate the heart. Anger easily leads to murder.

---

[1] Heb. 11:1-2, 4.
[2] Heb. 11:6.
[3] Gen. 4:3-5.

This connection between anger and murder was specifically identified by Jesus in His most famous sermon.[1] And the apostle Paul picked up that same theme and emphasized that anger gives Satan a foothold in man's soul to wreak havoc.[2] It certainly did that in Cain's life.

It is events and circumstances like this one that open the door for prodigals to depart on a journey. Whether it is guilt or shame or some other motivation that is driving them away to a far country, they need to remember that the Father of all grace, mercy, and love is standing on the porch waiting for them to return so He can pour out His love and forgiveness upon them.

Seth, the second Abel?

Seth took the place of his dead brother Abel as a righteous man who walked with God in faith. Adam had Seth when he was one hundred years old. He then lived eight hundred more years and had other sons and daughters, but these either became like Cain or like Seth so their histories are not emphasized.

Until Cain moved away with his clan from the presence of the Lord, we have no reason in the text of Genesis to think that any of the descendants of Adam and Eve had completely failed to respond to the God of creation. If it is supposed that there had to be many who did not believe in God, it should be recognized that this view is not the assumption that the Scriptures themselves make. Many today are more comfortable holding the assumption that most of Adam and Eve's descendants did not believe in the one, true God of creation. But the Bible leads us in the opposite direction.

---

[1] Matt. 5:21-26.
[2] Eph. 4:25-27.

What is clear is that only Seth's descendants are explicitly said to have "called upon the name of the Lord." This kind of dependent responsiveness is never ascribed to any of Cain's descendants. Consequently, the Bible leads us to assume that they didn't call upon the Lord. This does not mean they did not believe in the Lord; it only means that in times of crises they lived as prodigals, not devoted to or dependent upon their heavenly Father. They relied upon themselves rather than God.

...

*Evangelism simply is not a part of the paradigm
the Bible sets before its readers.*

...

As these generations from Adam to Noah are surveyed, it is noteworthy that for well over one thousand years there was no mention of evangelism. This omission of evangelism is consistent with the real storyline of the Bible, namely, that those listed in the Biblical record until the time of the great flood had already believed in the God of creation but had not responded faithfully to Him. They lived a prodigal life, some at home and some abroad. Consequently, God was dealing with individuals who needed to straighten their lives out; He was calling people to repent, to return to Him, and to walk righteously by faith. God's heart was broken because they refused His love and forgiveness.[1]

...

*God was grieved over the wickedness
resulting from estrangement from Him.*

...

---

[1] Gen. 6:5-6.

He did not refer to these wicked people as eternally damned or eternally lost, or unsaved, or unredeemed persons (in the traditional sense of those terms). In fact, the possibility of hell is never brought up as a warning to the wicked. Rather, God is indirectly comparing all the wicked people to Noah and the righteousness that he displayed practically.

> "And the Lord was sorry that He had made man on the earth, and He was grieved in His heart. . . But Noah found favor in the eyes of the Lord. . . . ***Noah was a righteous man, blameless in his time; Noah walked with God.***" (Gen. 6:6, 8, 9, emphases mine)

The point that God was making through Moses is that Noah was *righteous* while the others living in his day were *unrighteous*. He walked with God; the others did not. Moses is not comparing Noah who was *saved* to the rest of the world who were *lost* (in the traditional sense of those terms). The Bible gives the reader no reason to interpret its narrative as a believer/unbeliever issue or a saved/lost issue or a heaven/hell issue. To make it such is to assume ideas that were not being described by the inspired author. Moses was only contrasting wickedness to righteousness, and nothing more.[1]

...

Even in the face of universal wickedness, God did not call for the godly line to evangelize the ungodly line.

...

If one looks through the stained glass window of sacred, historical theology, he will only see what those before him had seen. Their window is not transparent, letting the reader see what is on the other side. Their window only portrays the conclusions that have already been etched into the windowpane.

---

[1] Cf., Ps. 1:1-6. This psalm should be used as an introduction to the whole Bible.

The issue in Genesis clearly concerns living righteously rather than living wickedly. It is not a heaven versus hell issue. Consequently, instead of assuming that those who were drowned in the flood did not know God, the opposite is most assuredly the truth. They all knew God from His own revelation of Himself to them.[1] They all had a relationship with Him even though they sinned flagrantly.

God was disciplining His prodigal sons and daughters in the flood. The discipline was justified because they were wasting their lives and leading those around them to do the same.

...

Being one who believed in the existence of the one, true God did not shield him from God's temporal judgment.

...

The worst thing in the world is to stray so far from God that He determines it wise to remove that person from this earthly life! While God is both loving and patient, there comes a time when His patience is replaced with righteous wrath. As long as a person has breath, the grace, love, and mercy of God are still being offered.

---

[1] Rom. 1:18-20.

Chapter 4

Noah

In keeping with Jesus' *Parable of the Prodigal Son*, Noah is the next *son*, or family member, and major character in the drama contained in God's Word. He must have been a great man of God. He is identified as a righteous man in a day when evil and corruption seemed to be the norm. In one way, we might think of him as representing the diametrical opposite to Adam[1] and Eve. They had a perfect environment but sinned anyway. Noah, on the other hand, lived in a grossly wicked society, but walked with God righteously.

Noah's environment was so evil that God became grieved over the matter. He reached the point where He was sorry that He had made man in the first place. Unfortunately, God's chosen people will reproduce this same grievous situation later on in the history that followed. So, both before the flood and after it, God has given us two situations that clearly demonstrate that those who believe in God can be so corrupt that God may want to remove them from the earth.[2]

But with Noah, God was delighted. His responsiveness to God was such that it brought him favor from the Lord.[3] But we should note that his *initial* faith in God is never discussed nor is

---

[1] Adam died roughly 60 years before the birth of Noah. Consequently, his influence would have been extensive or at least it had the opportunity of being so.
[2] Relate these passages to each other: Ex. 4:22-23; 14:31; 15:9, 13; 19:5-6; 32:1-10.
[3] Gen. 6:8. Cf., again Heb. 11:1-2, 6.

it assumed to reflect some grand transition from an eternally lost state to an eternally saved state. He is simply presented as a creature who walked with his Creator.

We ought to be genuinely intrigued by the fact that God is telling us that Noah was the *only* righteous person living in his generation. The phrase, translated "in this time" by the NASB, literally means "generation," and should be taken in this context for a period well over one hundred years.[1] That he *alone*[2] was righteous in his day the context seems to demand since *God was looking for people to save from the flood.*[3] But He did not find any besides Noah and his family. If there were other righteous people, God would have brought them into the ark as well. That there weren't any others is clearly stated in the context.[4]

The Bible presents its readers with the paradigm of prodigals. So when we see them, we must understand that they are "sons" who have gone astray. What God is seeking from these individuals is repentance and a return to a walk of communion with Him that produces practical righteousness. That is the window through which the Scriptures can be understood properly.

...

*Practical righteousness alone stays God's judgment
or delivers one from it.*

...

We are forced to ask the obvious question, "What happened to the rest of *the godly line* coming from Seth who 'called upon the name of the Lord?'" When we remember how long people

---

[1] Gen. 5:32; 6:8-9; 7:1.
[2] Gen. 7:1.
[3] Gen. 6:11-12; 7:1. God *looked* for others; He scanned the earth of others.
[4] Gen. 6:12-13.

NOAH

lived back then, we are *forced* to conclude that those who knew God didn't do a very good job of raising their children in the nurture and admonition of the Lord. We are also led to conclude that their children, those who were well grounded in their belief in the God of creation, did not persevere in righteousness. Let me state the obvious in a slightly different way: *no one at this time was persevering in his faith except Noah.*

Only Noah was walking with God consistently.

To assume that Noah was the only one who believed in the God of creation at the time is to stray from the *assumption* that the Bible itself presents. The one who has assuredly believed in the one, true God may, nevertheless, live wickedly and suffer God's chastisement for it. That is the plain message of the flood.

...

Persevering in righteous living is not guaranteed to anyone.

...

And even with respect to Cain's line, the reader is nowhere *forced* to conclude that his line did not have anyone in it that had believed in the God who had created him. The same corrupt behavior, that Cain's line exhibited, can be also presumed in the entire godly line of Seth. Why? Because there was no righteousness found in them at the time of Noah. *So apparently Seth's line had no better walk with God than Cain's line had.*

Enoch, one of Seth's descendants, had such a walk with God that God, apparently, couldn't wait for him to get to heaven. So one day He just "snatched him up" to heaven. *Enoch was the man that God had hoped Adam would have been from the moment of his creation.* Enoch must have done a marvelous job of raising his son, Methuselah, and his grandson, Lamech even though these men, in their turn, didn't produce the godly heritage expected.

To my best calculation, the heads of the families from Methuselah to Noah were present to impact all the succeeding generations up to the time Noah is commissioned to begin building the ark. That is a lot of spiritual maturity to have present with so little influence coming from it!

Once again we have to notice that nowhere in the story of Adam's succeeding generations is there a movement to evangelize others.[1] This is true all the way to the time of the great flood. *It seems rather plain that a person could know God without worshipping Him as the God that He is.*[2]

This is a principle flowing naturally out of the paradigm of the *Parable of the Prodigal Son*. God had many sons, but only some, and in Noah's case only one, chose to walk with Him; the others became prodigals either at home or abroad.

The paradigm of the *Parable of the Prodigal Son* is a model that explains how God's family is experiencing fracture because of sin. The Father is patiently waiting for His children to return to Him so that He can pour out His love, forgiveness, and blessings upon them. God's runaways, though living in a distant country, are still His sons.

This is the paradigm the Bible urges us to use to understand its message. This is the paradigm that Noah and the Great Flood present to us. There is no need to read into it what is not there.

---

[1] The apostle Peter tells us that Noah was a "herald" of righteousness (2Pet. 2:5). Since God was looking for practical righteousness in the lives of His children, being a herald of what God was seeking certainly makes a lot of sense.

[2] Cf., Rom. 1:18-32.

Chapter 5

Abraham

After the flood man began to multiply once again. Yet, instead of spreading out over the whole earth, they remained together as they migrated eastward. When they arrived at a plain in the land of Shinar, they decided to settle there together. In fact, they attempted to establish at the tower of Babel a perversion of God's original plan for ruling over the earth.

God responded to their disobedience by forcing a division among the people by changing their languages. This limited their ability to communicate with each other. Being unable to communicate in the building project that they had begun for their own glory and permanence, man had to disperse from there by groups, forming nations according to the language they now possessed.

Out of all the people then living, God focused on one man. His name was Abraham. While the Bible assumes that God had some kind of connection or relationship with all the descendants of Noah and his three sons, God chose this man with whom He would make a covenant and promise many additional blessings. All that He promised Abraham and his descendants demonstrated that God's plan was still *earth-centered*; it was about life lived now, about life lived upon this earth, rather than any concept of life lived in the hereafter. Life continued to be about representing God now in all that man did as they had fellowship with Him. There is still no promise of an eternal, heavenly destiny nor of any method by which such a destiny might be obtained. Until now, the only prophecy that God had given to man described a special seed of woman who was to come and handle Satan, the great tempter and deceiver of mankind. Now God makes some promises to Abraham and confirms those promises with a covenant that illumines the path that history will walk.

Abraham is the key to several major issues raised in the Bible. But by far, the most important may be what Abraham teaches us about the doctrine of justification. The key passage explaining Abraham's justification are Gen. 15:6 and Gen. 22:1-18 (which is explained for us by James, the half-brother of Jesus).

If this passage accurately describes Abraham's justification, and it does, then no theological system has the right to set forth any other formulation of that doctrine than what is described here. The apostle Paul and James certainly were convinced of this when they used these precise passages to teach the doctrine of justification in their letters to other believers. And Paul made it clear that no other concept of justification will ever be warranted.[1]

...

*The correct understanding of Gen. 15:6
will radically change the way the Bible is interpreted.*

...

In theological circles the doctrine of justification is sometimes said to be the tenet by which the Christian church stands or falls.[2] Over the course of church history this doctrine has been the topic of great debates that seem to have no end.

---

[1] Rom. 4:22-25.
[2] N.T. Wright, *Justification, God's plan and Paul's vision*, p. 46. Here Wright suggests that John Piper, in his book *The Future of Justification* (p. 37), sees the doctrine of justification,

Of the many questions of critical importance surrounding the discussion of justification, here are some that are pertinent to our study:

- Does Paul or James use *justification* (and the verb *justify*) to refer to man's *initial trust in God*?
- Does justification result in a person's forgiveness of past sins and in Christ's righteousness being *"imputed"* (i.e., being *given*) to him?
- Does *justification* refer to God's declaration that a person is now in a *legally obtained, permanent "right standing"* that secures his eternal, heavenly destiny?

I was taught to answer all of these questions in the affirmative. But do these points really give us the true intent of this crucial, theologically loaded term? Or is it possible that we might have been following an interpretative suggestion that has clouded rather than clarified the Scriptures? Just because a theology may be coherent or has a long history of acceptance and propagation, doesn't thereby make that theology Biblical. After studying the history of the debate over justification for twenty-five years, Alister E. McGrath concluded that, at a minimum,

> "Justification cannot be regarded as the centre of Paul's thought, nor of Christianity. . . . **systematic theology has lost its moorings in the Bible**, and prefers to conduct its disputes with reference to systematic theologians of the past, rather than by direct engagement with biblical texts."[1] (emphasis mine)

---

as it was developed by Augustine and preached for fifteen hundred years, as so central to Christianity that should it ever be set aside, Christianity would be too. Internationally respected authors such as Wright and Alister McGrath are suggesting that work needs to be done on the topic of justification. With that I am in complete agreement.

[1] Alister E. McGrath, *The History of the Christian Doctrine of Justification*, Third Edition, Cambridge University Press, New York; vol. I, p. 420

It should be obvious that if we can determine what Abraham's justification refers to in Gen. 15:6 and in Gen. 22:1-18, then we can obtain enormous help in understanding what justification means both in the OT as well as in the NT. The conclusion of our study on this topic will lead us right back to the Prodigal Paradigm and establish its validity.

Once we discover the distinctions between a person's *supposed initial acceptance* by God, identified by theologians as his justification, or as his salvation in other texts, we can determine with confidence the spiritual state of the people being addressed both in the OT and in the Gospels of the NT. Could it be that much of our confusion in understanding the message of the Bible has been due to the fact that we have misidentified or mischaracterized the addressees? And could it be that we have made this mistake because we have been looking through the wrong window into the Scriptures?

Abraham: the original heathen in Africa?

As we investigate Abraham's life back in Ur of the Chaldeans, we come across the unfortunate fact that much of the circumstances that orchestrated Abraham's walk with God remain hidden in obscurity. We know that he came from Ur of the Chaldeans, but there is no unanimity among scholars concerning the location of Ur either as a city or as a land[1] in which Chaldeans lived. We know almost nothing of Abraham's life before his calling except for the comment found in Joshua 24:2-3, which says,

---

[1] Cf., Acts 7:2, 4. Stephen speaks not of Ur but of "the land" of the Chaldeans and located this land in Mesopotamia.

> "And Joshua said to all the people, 'Thus says the Lord the God of Israel, "From ancient times your fathers lived beyond the River, namely, **Terah**, the father of **Abraham** and ... of **Nabor**, and **they served others gods**. Then **I took** your father Abraham from beyond the River, **and led** him through all the land of Canaan, and multiplied his descendants and gave him Isaac."'" (emphases mine)

From this historical statement, we learn that Abraham had once "served other gods." But the text doesn't tell us when his polytheistic views developed. Was it *before* he began to walk with the one, true God or *afterwards*? Even though he was a polytheist, I find it interesting that this text, along with the entirety of the OT, leaves it a mystery as to what exactly was involved in God "taking" Abraham and "leading" him after He had called him to go to the land of Canaan. I believe we ought not miss the simplicity of this statement nor be tempted, as we are taught to do, to read into the text all the theology that we think ought to be here.

It is impossible to affirm with any kind of certainty whether Abraham's response to his initial calling by God was his initial faith in the one, true God. Abraham's calling was to go to a land that he had not seen and dwell there. It wasn't a calling to initially come to God in faith. Consequently, it seems highly unlikely that Abraham's response to God's calling had anything to do with an initial response to God. And if that is true, then Abraham's response to God's calling couldn't have been his justification by God (if we continue to understand justification in its traditional, theological sense).

It seems much more likely that God's calling was given to Abraham as a responsive believer. He could be called a believer because he possessed a vital faith in God, a faith that manifested itself in a righteous walk. Because of such a faith, God chose him for further service, exactly like He did with a Pharisee in the NT named Saul. The later history of God's people demonstrates conclusively that a person can believe in the one, true God and walk with Him, howbeit inconsistently, even while he worships other gods at the same time. But there is no contextual reason to identify Abraham's response to God's call as initial faith.[1]

The exact, religious beliefs of Abraham's family are as uncertain as is the exact location in which his family had lived. All the families of the earth at that time came from the same family: *Noah's three sons*. It is also interesting that Shem lived for over two hundred years after the ninth generation of his descendants were born. I am suggesting that the *Book of Genesis* leads us to believe that Shem might have had an enormous impact upon his descendants. By surviving a world-wide flood that killed everyone else on the planet and continuing to worship the God who had brought that flood upon mankind, Shem would have given a testimony to God's greatness that would have created reverence in every heart.

...

We must not assume that because there is idolatry or polytheism involved in a person's life, he couldn't have believed in the one, true God and walked with Him.

...

While Abraham may have been an idolater as he was a polytheist, he still worshipped the one, true God along with those other so-called gods. If Solomon, the smartest man to ever walk upon this earth besides Jesus, fell into this exact error, it is likely that others who had responded to God in faith during

---

[1] It is almost a certainty that the term "call" is never used to describe initial faith.

their lives could have been just as double-minded. These have never been mutually exclusive issues in the Bible even though it is commonly taught that they are so in many theological circles.

As far as Abraham's faith and justification are concerned, the crucial text before us simply says that Abraham . . .

> "*believed in the Lord*; and He *reckoned* it [Abraham's faith] to him *as* [or *for*] righteousness." (Gen. 15:6, emphasis and brackets mine)

God *reckoned* Abraham's response of faith *as* righteousness. In Pauline terms, Abraham believed in the Lord, and the Lord God accounted him *justified* as a result of that belief. To be *justified* or to be *accounted just* is the same thing as being *declared* (not made) *righteous*. These points are generally agreed upon by most interpreters. Now let's dig a bit deeper.

...

*The Messiah, what precious little that had been revealed about Him by this time in history, was **not** the object of Abraham's faith or included in it in any way as far as we know.*

...

What is the immediate context of Gen. 15? What are the options (if there are any) to understanding the text as it stands? The student of Scripture has the right to equate Gen. 15:6 with justification because Paul does it in his discussion of justification in the fourth chapter of Romans. Paul tells us that the *justification* being described here is literally translated as "God *accounts* or *reckons* Abraham's *faith* **as** *righteousness*."[1]

This accounting or reckoning on the part of God could be His evaluation of a previous response by Abraham[2] or it could

---

[1] Rom. 4:5, 9.
[2] Allen P. Ross, *Creation and Blessing*, a guide to the study and exposition of Genesis, Baker Books, Grand Rapids, Michigan, 1998, pp. 309-10.

be God's evaluation of a present response by Abraham.[1] It appears to me that the only significant reason for understanding Gen. 15:6 as a past event and not as a present response is the *presumption* that "God's reckoning of Abraham's faith for righteousness" must be taken to describe his ***initial*** belief in God. In other words, theology drives the interpretation that Gen. 15:6 describes a previous response given by Abraham when he was living in Ur before God ever called him to leave there.

You see, most theologies teach us that it is at ***initial belief*** in God that justification takes place. Most who hold to this view *suppose* they are following the apostle Paul's argument in Romans 3:21–4:25. While Paul definitively called what happened to Abraham in Gen. 15:6 "justification," he nowhere affirmed that it happened at the moment Abraham *first* believed in God.

Based upon the *assumption* that the event in Gen. 15:6 describes Abraham's *initial* faith, our systematic theologies *assume* that this declaration by God of justification signifies Abraham's initial forgiveness of all of his sins, his obtainment of "imputed righteousness" from God (giving him the positive righteousness of Christ), and the guarantee of his eternal, heavenly destiny.

But how do we know these things are true?

How do we know that a person is forgiven for all of his sins at the moment of his initial faith in God?

How do we know that he receives "a righteousness from God" (presumed to be the actual righteousness of Jesus Christ

---

[1] Bruce K. Waltke, *Genesis*, a commentary, Zondervan, Grand Rapids, Michigan, 2001, p. 242.

that is imputed or given to the person the moment he initially believes)?

How do we know it is *at this justification* that his eternal destiny is secured forever?

Can these *assumptions* be proven? Are they the clear statements of Scripture?

The answer that I have come to is a resounding "No! These *assumptions* cannot be proven from clear statements in the Scriptures themselves." It appears to me that these doctrines are *assumed to be true* because they follow a certain logic or theological synthesis, formulated by men (who probably loved God deeply, but nevertheless who have erred in their construct of the issues that the Bible sets forth).

They were looking through the wrong window into the Scriptures. Theirs was the stained glass of Augustine's fourth century church and of the Reformers' great cathedrals. *When we use the wrong paradigm or template to understand the Bible, we see only what our theology has preconditioned us to see.*

The doctrinal connections between justification, initial faith, forgiveness, and the gift of Christ's righteousness can't actually be demonstrated to be true from *explicit* statements of Scripture. So, we must ask ourselves this question: are we going to be more persuaded by theology or what the Scriptures *explicitly* teach? The former is a whole lot easier than the latter, but the latter is always the safer approach.

The sufficiency of natural revelation

So, if Gen. 15:6 doesn't refer to Abraham's *initial* faith in God, we naturally wonder what exactly were the circumstances when Abraham initially came to faith in Yahweh? And what were the means that God used to draw him? If Abraham did not have any oral tradition to believe, which supposition is assuredly not true, or if he had not had any personal encounter with God, either in a vision or from personal experience, would God's revelation of Himself in natural creation be enough information, if believed, to bring him into a dependent relationship with God?

Many say, "No." That was the opinion that I was taught in seminary. But is that denial clearly taught in the Scriptures themselves? Or does that denial actually spring from a *presumption* about what *the content of faith must necessarily include*? It is most definitely the latter.[1] God has not left any man without a sufficient witness.[2]

Psalm 19:1-4 tell us that . . .

> "The heavens are telling of **the glory of God**; And their expanse is declaring **the work of His hands**. Day to day pours forth **speech**, And night to night reveals **knowledge**. There is no speech, nor are there words; Their voice is not heard. Their line has gone out **through all the earth**, And their utterances to **the end of the world**." (emphases mine)

This revelation of God displayed in nature presents something of God's glory (or personal attributes[3]) to each and every person living in the world. *God's natural creation, therefore, explains something of what He is like.*

Furthermore, this revelation is *clear* because God Himself is doing the revealing; it is *effective* because God Himself has laid

---

[1] It is *presumed* that people in the OT had to believe in the coming Messiah and in His death for sins and His resurrection from the dead. Since this information is not given in natural creation, believing in the revelation God gives in nature will prove to be inadequate. The question is simple: "Is this *presumption* about the content of faith true?"
[2] Cf., Acts 14:14-17.
[3] E.g., see Ex. 33:17–34:9 for a list of some of God's attributes.

this revelation before every man so that he clearly understands, from what has been made, that he is accountable to Him, the only true God. This is precisely what Paul said in his letter to the Roman Churches in Rom. 1:18-19:

> "For the wrath of God is being revealed from heaven against all ungodliness and unrighteousness of men, who suppress **the truth** in unrighteousness, because *that which is known about God is evident* within them; for *God* made it *evident* to them."

...
A limited revelation would require a commensurate belief.
...

God's revelation of Himself in nature includes His eternal power and His divine providence,[1] His righteous nature,[2] and man's accountability to this God and to no other.[3] God has left Himself with a witness in nature around man,[4] and it is drawing him to God by convincing him of His goodness, power, and right to rule over him. That conviction is necessarily accompanied by the persuasion that man is, therefore, accountable to the God who is revealing Himself. Man is, then, as Paul clearly and authoritatively explained, "without excuse."

The basis for the relationship between God and Abraham is a very simple one. Abraham responded to whatever God was revealing, regardless of how much or how little it was. Abraham must not be required to believe what had not yet been revealed to him.[5] His responsibility was circumscribed by the revelation that he had at that time.

---

[1] Rom. 1:20.
[2] Ps. 50:6; 97:6.
[3] Rom. 1:20; Ps. 97:7-9.
[4] Acts 14:8-18. His witness is identified as rains and good crops.
[5] Acts 10:14-15; John 15:22-25.

What exactly did he believe in order for him to become one of God's *sons*? That actually is the wrong question!

Nowhere throughout the entire OT is there ever a scenario in which a person is identified with a group of people who are called *unbelievers* but who becomes a *believer* by expressing a newly found faith in God.

Nowhere is a person portrayed as someone who is condemned to hell but then obtains salvation from hell by his new faith in God.

Nowhere is God describing anyone as a person who did not belong to Him.

The entire Bible is about the creatures' duty and privilege of fulfilling the purpose for which they were made: *ruling for God on this earth as they maintained fellowship with God*. Some represent God well; others not so much. When divine discipline arises, it should not be a surprise.

…

The whole Bible is about service.

…

This is the *Paradigm of the Prodigal Son*. Both the lovingkindness of God[1] and the severe discipline by God[2] come upon mankind for a remedial goal: to draw man back into a loving intimacy with the Father. God only judges those who have earned it and need it to return to Him.

This is the window that the reader must look through to understand the Bible properly. This is the paradigm that will explain best what God is doing throughout the Bible and in the world today.

---

[1] Cf., Rom. 2:4.
[2] Cf., Heb. 12:4-12.

Abraham believes in God, becomes a useful son

God made Himself known to Abraham, and Abraham believed whatever God had made known to him. What means God used to communicate truth about Himself to Abraham is left undisclosed. At what age this communication first took place and Abraham first began to respond in faith, we are not told. *But by responding to God, he became a useful son to God.* And this relationship led God to call him out of Ur *at least ten years before* the scene that describes his justification for us in Gen. 15:6.

…
The reckoning of righteousness is repetitive in a person's life.
…

When a person believed in God, *each time he believed God*, he was accounted or accepted as righteous. And God became his God in those moments in a practical, personal sense. He became a part of God's people who were *useful* to God in those moments. In this sense alone, God designated the entire nation of Israel as *His son* in the OT.

To **believe in** God and to **believe God** are the same thing. There is no difference between believing in God's ability and faithfulness to do what He promises and believing God when He promises to accept as righteous the man who trusts in Him.

…
When a person believes God's promise,
he is believing in the God who has made the promise.
…

In my first draft of this book I dealt with Gen. 15:6 in the way I had been taught, namely, *supposing that this verse basically described Abraham's **initial faith** in God* and, was, consequently, giving God's resultant declaration of his righteous standing or status before Him. This, I was taught, is what the Bible describes as *justification by faith*.

Now I believe that conclusion is very wide of the mark. *A person's **initial** response of faith in God is **never** even recognized or isolated in all of the OT and was certainly **never** meant to be the focus of attention for the reader or student of Scripture.* It is, therefore, conjectural to espouse the view that initial faith turns a person into a *son of God*. The assumption of Scripture, in complete agreement with the *Parable of the Prodigal Son*, is that *all men are sons, but they become useful in fulfilling God's original commission of them only when they are living by faith in God.*

...

*Initial faith in God was **never** analyzed and dogmatized, as we have done today, by calling it **justification by faith**.*

...

A useful son is one who walks in fellowship with God as he represents God in all that he does. And as he walks by faith, God is molding him into an effective ruler. Rulership in the coming earthly kingdom of Messiah is the inheritance that he can gain by being a good representative of God now through righteous living.

For the most part, the people in the OT only had one option. They had to choose how they were going to respond to the God who was revealing Himself to them. They had to choose how or whether they would trust Him for help to deal with the trials presently confronting them. They were not concerned about the future; they were not asking what they needed to do to go to heaven and to escape hell; they were not deliberating over a coming Messiah. They were vitally concerned about their present circumstances and how they were going to survive their present trial. Even the most superficial reading of the OT confirms this analysis completely.

The reader of the OT basically gets the idea that life for the Israelite was, indeed, *a father-son affair*. The son would periodically become rebellious, turn away from God his father, and go his own way. God would allow that rebellion for a time and then bring some type of temporal trial or judgment upon that son to bring him to his senses. Then the son would eventually cry out for mercy, and God would either deliver him directly or raise up a deliverer from the midst of the people.

Not all of God's overtures were effective in bringing about the son's repentance. Consequently, some died in the midst of the discipline; others died in faraway lands before ever coming to their senses. And still others stayed at home, "kept the faith" in a ritualistic sense, but did not make themselves useful to God by developing a vital relationship with Him.

In Gen. 15 we move ten years, at least, into Abraham's walk with God from the time God had called him for special service. And in this context, Abraham believed what God had revealed for him to believe, namely, that God would give him a multitudinous lineage. This faith-response found approval with God,[1] or, to use the Apostle Paul's words, this faith-response was sufficient for his *justification*.[2]

In Abraham's justification God declared him righteous because He reckoned Abraham's faith *as* righteousness. Abraham did not *become* righteous at that moment; he was not *given* a righteousness from someone else (namely, Christ); his

---

[1] Heb. 11:2.
[2] Rom. 4:1-8, 18-25.

own faith-response was *declared to be* (or taken *for*) righteousness. In other words, God declared that Abraham's receptiveness to His promise of a multitudinous progeny, a simple response of faith that involved no act of his will afterward,[1] met His demands and, therefore, could be declared a righteous response.

It is Abraham's faith that is *reckoned, imputed,* and *taken for* righteousness. He is not given someone else's righteousness because that was not a need he had at this moment or at any moment in his life. This passage describes Abraham's responsiveness to God, not his trial before God. Abraham is blessed because of his response not because of God's mercy and grace shown to him when he *supposedly* couldn't respond because he was dead in his trespasses and sins as the old paradigm would have us believe. God is declaring what Abraham was offering to Him righteous. God is not offering to give Abraham a righteousness that he *supposedly* needed so he could be righteous before Him forever and gain a heavenly destiny. Rather, God declared that Abraham gave the right response, a response of faith, that He was looking for, and it pleased Him.

The situation described in Gen. 15:1-6 simply had nothing to do with Abraham's initial faith in God. And if it had nothing to do with initial faith, it does not support the traditional understanding of justification by faith. *We have been guilty of filling the term **justification** with meaning that the Bible does not place upon it.*

We don't know what God revealed to a person in OT times, nor how much He required that person to believe at his initial

---

[1] Gen. 15:5 does suggest that Abraham had to do some things *before* he believed though.

moment of faith (if there were such a moment). **The OT doesn't cover those issues**. But we may suspect that when God revealed Himself to a person, that person was held accountable to believe the revelation that God was providing him. Since God is the one determining the content of the revelation, we can be sure that enough was revealed to each person for him to be acceptable to God if he believed it and acted according to it.

Abraham's walk was justified by God

The apostle Paul picked up the subject of Abraham's justification in Gen. 15:6 and wrote a little discourse on it in his letter to the assemblies in Rome. Neither Paul nor the rest of the NT gives justification a new twist or an added meaning to that given in Gen. 15:6.

...

The apostle Paul tells us that justification is whatever happened to Abraham in Gen. 15:6.

...

Paul made it clear from Romans 4:22-24 that justification certainly did not change into something entirely different from what had occurred in Abraham's life as Moses recorded it for us in Gen. 15:6.

...

Paul used Abraham's justification as the template for all others, regardless of whether they lived before the cross of Jesus or after it.

...

Writing under the inspiration of the Holy Spirit over 20 years after Jesus' death and resurrection, Paul said in Romans 4:22-24,

> "Therefore also it [Abraham's faith in God] was reckoned to him as righteousness. Now **not for his sake only** was it written, that it was reckoned to him, but **for our sake also**, to whom it will be reckoned, as **those who believed in Him** [i.e., God the Father] **who raised Jesus our Lord from the dead**." (emphases and brackets mine)

Here he explicitly told the Roman Christians that they were *justified* in exactly the same way that Abraham had been *justified*. The coming of Jesus, the death and resurrection of Jesus, the ascension of Jesus, and the beginning of the Church did not change in the slightest way how a person is justified or what happens in justification. Consequently, what are we to conclude from these facts?

...

Justification describes something that is occurring to those who are walking with God!

...

Justification does not mark the moment of transition from being the proverbial *unbeliever* to being a *believer*, from being unforgiven to being forgiven, from being hell bound to being heaven bound. *Justification is God's declaration upon **a believing man's walk**, not upon **the pagan man's initial** (and, what is wrongly called, saving) **faith**.* In justification God is approving of a believer's walk; He is declaring that the believer is walking righteously. Conversely, the one who has turned away from God to follow his own desires is being temporally judged (or condemned) for his sin.

Jesus didn't come to be a game changer; He came as a game fulfiller. He came to fulfill the will of the Father so that the Father would be just in justifying those who walk in faith. Many have misunderstood what Paul was saying in Rom. 3:24-26 when he specifically related justification to having faith in Jesus.[1] With this misunderstanding, they confidently read their mistaken ideas back into the OT passage of Gen. 15:6. So, Abraham had to have believed in the coming Messiah because justification only comes to those who do. Isn't that what Rom. 3:26 requires?

But Paul's fuller explanation of the faith in Jesus that results in justification is given in Gal. 2:20 where he described it more fully this way:

> "I have been crucified with Christ; and it is no longer I who live, but Christ lives in me; and *the life which I now live in the flesh I live by faith in the Son of God* who loved me and delivered Himself up for me." (emphases mine)

Justification is not a permanent standing of righteousness that results from a once-for-all trust in Jesus. *Rather, God's justifying work occurs every time a person walks by faith.* Obviously this faith walk is a repetitive occurrence, taking place each day throughout a person's whole life.

Whenever his walk was not one of trusting in God (in the OT) or in Jesus (in the NT), God could not justify (approve of in any way) his responses. In those times, if God were asked, "How can You justify that person's actions?" God would respond, "I can't." Consequently, over those actions the person will never hear the divine commendation, "Well done, good and faithful servant." Once God has pronounced His approval, no one will ever be able to bring a viable charge against those actions thus approved[2]. If God declared those actions to be

---

[1] Rom. 3:26.
[2] Rom. 8:31-34. This is what these verses clearly state to be the case and it ought to force the interpreter back to verses 29-30 to be consistent in his thinking.

righteous, they were, and no one will ever be able to prove they weren't. And if He pronounced their actions unrighteous, no one will ever overturn that evaluation either.

The storyline of the Bible describes individuals who have been created in the image of God. Each one's purpose is to represent God in all of the situations that he encounters throughout his life. But because of indwelling sin, the result of man's first sin, he needs to be encouraged, enticed, warned, and even goaded to walk with God in all holiness. This, once again, is the reason that the *Parable of the Prodigal Son* fits as the template for understanding the storyline of the Bible. The message of the Bible is not about becoming a son; it is about becoming a *useful* son, a son that fulfills God's original commission for all men who would ever come into the world. God created each person to handle every day that had been ordained for him to live. He makes sure that no temptation ever comes into a person's life that he is not able to successfully face if he trusts in His grace.

Chapter 6

Abraham to Moses

As we consider Abraham's son, Isaac, and Isaac's son, Jacob, and Jacob's twelve sons, who become the heads of the twelve tribes of the nation of Israel, we must realize that, as in the case of all the individuals who preceded them or who will follow them, *the Bible will assume some level of relationship with the one, true God who had revealed Himself to them*. This assumption, that a relationship with God was already existent, will then be verified as their interactions with God are set before the reader. The reader should not expect to ever find one example of initial faith in any of the records of the patriarchs' lives.

Since the Bible doesn't emphasize that event, why should we?

Since the Bible doesn't mention that event, why should we look for it until we at last find it because we've read it into the storyline ourselves?

Isaac believes in God, becomes a useful son

Isaac is mentioned one hundred and thirty-two times in the Bible. There are 113 references to him in the OT and 19 in the NT (six times in the formula: Abraham, Isaac and Jacob; six times in references to his line of descent). Those six references to the formula of Abraham, Isaac, and Jacob are probably the most

THE PRODIGAL PARADIGM

important because *they ultimately establish Isaac's faith in God as well as his faithful walk with God.*

We begin to see Isaac's faith displayed in his life when he prayed to the Lord on behalf of his wife who was barren.[1] God heard his prayer, another indication of Isaac's spiritual condition, and Rebekah conceived.

So Isaac prayed to God, and God heard him. But according to the Bible, God doesn't hear sinners.[2] Hence, we are right to assume, as the Bible does, that Isaac had a relationship with God, and was walking with Him at the time of his prayer.

The same can be said for Isaac's wife, Rebekah. Rebekah had trouble in her pregnancy and prayed to the Lord, and the Lord explained to her why she was having trouble in carrying her twins.[3] Communication went both ways. This certainly establishes the fact that a relationship did exist.

But there is more ...

We find that the Lord actually appeared to Isaac to confirm the Abrahamic Covenant to him. During this personal encounter with God, He commanded him to remain in the land and not to go down to Egypt even though there was a famine where he lived.[4] Then the Lord appeared to Isaac a second time at Beersheba, declaring,

> "*I am the God of your father Abraham*; Do not fear, *for I am with you. I will bless you*, and multiply your descendants, for the sake of My Servant Abraham." (Gen. 26:24, emphasis mine)

Isaac responded to this revelation of God by building an altar at Beersheba and by "calling upon the name of the Lord."

---

[1] Gen. 25:21.
[2] See Psalm 66:18; Proverbs 1:28-33; Isaiah 1:15; John 9:31
[3] Gen. 25:22-23.
[4] Gen. 26:1-6.

Isaac had been walking with God and worshiping Him long before he called upon the name of the Lord. The same God, in whom Abraham had believed, was guiding, protecting, and promising to bless Isaac. And the blessings were so abundant that even those who hated him admitted that "the Lord had been with him."[1] God's presence with a person is never an idle presence; it is always purposeful; it is always accomplishing what He had previously promised to do for the person who walked by faith.

…

*Only those who are already walking with God
have the privilege of calling upon the name of the Lord.*

…

When Isaac finally came to bless his sons, Jacob and Esau, he invoked God's goodness to bless them.[2] This indicates that Isaac communicated both his experiences with the God of his father Abraham and his belief in Him to both of his sons. This assumption is *explicitly* verified for the reader when Isaac's son, Jacob, left his family to remove himself from the anger of his brother Esau and to find a wife among his relatives. He journeyed as far as Beersheba before spending the night in sleep. Sometime in the night God appeared to him in a dream and said,

> "I am **the Lord, the God of your father Abraham and the God of Isaac**; the land on which you lie, I will give it to you and to your descendants." (Gen. 28:13, emphasis mine)

The God of Abraham was also the God of Isaac.

---

[1] Gen. 26:28.
[2] Gen. 27:27-29. Heb. 11:20 declares Isaac's act of blessing his sons an act of faith. This should be tied into Heb. 11:2, 6.

And just as Abraham's faith in the Lord was divinely declared as righteousness, it is consistent to believe that Isaac, having followed in Abraham's footsteps, reaped the same result.[1] This conclusion is a fact and not simply speculation since the NT tells us that he was a faithful believer who walked righteously with the Lord. Where does it tell us this? It tells us this each time it assures us that Isaac will be admitted into the promised Messianic Kingdom when it is finally set up at Jesus' Second Coming.[2] Apart from practical righteousness, the kind that only flows from a walk of faith, no one enters this promised kingdom.[3] Isaac must have been a faithful believer who walked with God because he will be in that future kingdom.

Understanding the OT's M.O., *modus operandi,* we know that Isaac had begun to respond at some point in his life to the God who had been disclosing Himself to him. But when exactly that was or what exactly he first believed is nowhere specified. And just as God had done with Abraham, He appeared more than once to Isaac personally, declaring for all generations that followed that He was Isaac's God as He had been Abraham's.

...

We ought to wonder whether the content of faith is as important as is the response of believing.

...

Yet from Cain to Isaac, God never even suggested that there was a certain content that a person had to believe as individuals began to

---

[1] Cf., Rom. 4:22-24. All persons from Abraham onward were justified the same way.
[2] Matt. 8:11; Lk. 13:28.
[3] Matt. 5:20; 7:21. His faith was reckoned for righteousness (Rom. 4:22-24). Cf., also: Isa. 45:24-25; 54:13-14; 60:14-15, 17-18, 20-21; 61:10-11; 62:1-5; 65:9-12. It is also suggested that the entire Book of Romans fits here. The theme of Romans is the need for practical righteousness to meet the condition for the Messiah to bring Israel's "salvation" to her (i.e., her kingdom).

respond to Him in faith. The emphasis of Scripture is, then, squarely upon their belief in Him rather than in a qualifying, established set of doctrines that needed to be believed. Doctrinal truth and a vital relationship with God are, most likely, two sides of the same coin. Both are needed, and they seem to be related proportionately. As one increases the other does also. But this applies only to a faith that is vital, living, or excellent, as Peter would describe it.[1] A person can increase in knowledge without increasing in faith, but he can't increase in faith without increasing in knowledge.

Jacob believes in God, becomes a useful son

Even in Jacob's grand deception of his father Isaac, he used God's goodness and His promises of personal blessings as the reasons he was able to find, kill, and prepare a meal so quickly from the game he was supposed to have just then killed.[2] It is evident that he possessed quite a significant belief in his father's God at that point. The blessing that is invoked upon Jacob by Isaac depends upon God's providence and bounty as well.[3] While he was just a child, Jacob had learned the truths about God's providence and His abundant provisions for the one who walked with Him. These truths were reinforced to him throughout the rest of his life as he experienced God's faithfulness toward him first hand.

And it is also reasonable to assume that Rebekah passed her faith on to her favorite son.[4] She could tell him of the time God had spoken to her when she labored to carry to full term the

---

[1] 2Pet. 1:5.
[2] Gen. 27:20.
[3] Gen. 27:27-29.
[4] Gen. 25:28.

twins that struggled in her womb. It was probably due to that divine revelation that she was motivated to deceive her husband in order to make certain that God's prediction over her twins came true. In the end Jacob received Isaac's blessing, and Esau was left to serve Jacob as God had predicted before they were born. Esau was the first born, but Jacob was born holding onto Esau's heel to symbolize his future supremacy of service to God over his brother.

On his journey back to his relatives to find a wife, Jacob had a dream. In it God appeared to him and said,

> "**I am the Lord, the God of your father Abraham and the God of Isaac**; the land on which you lie, I will give it to you and to your descendants. . . . And behold, I am **with** you, and **will keep** you wherever you go, and **will bring you back** to this land; for I **will not leave** you until I have done *what I have promised you*." (Gen. 28:13, 15, emphases mine)

God identified Himself as the God of his father Isaac. The God whom he had learned about from his father now manifested Himself personally to Jacob. In the dream, God promised His presence, His care, and Jacob's safe return to the land that He promised to give to him and to his descendants. That Jacob's dream-experience was a staggering one is seen from the comments he made when he awoke:

> "Surely *the Lord* is in this place, and I did not know it. . . . How awesome is this place! This is none other than *the house of God*, and this is the gate of heaven." (Gen. 28: 16, 17)

The vow that Jacob made that morning is not a vow to initially believe in the God of Abraham and Isaac. The record is unmistakable on that matter. Rather Jacob vowed to return a tithe (or tenth) of all that God supplied to him while he was on his journey.[1] He was basically saying, "If You provide for me as You say that You will, I'll return to You a portion of it for the rest of my life." Of course, Jacob would have had to maintain a similar sense of obligation to give back part of God's bounty to him as an offering to God for His goodness. And while the expectation of God's presence and provisions and Jacob's continuing sense of obligation to God are implicit here, they are *explicitly* confirmed later[2] as the Bible's M.O. consistently plays itself out to the reader's expectations.

...

Implicit in Jacob's vow is the requirement that Jacob would live with some expectation of God's presence with him as He provided for him the rest of his life.

...

After Jacob had been made rich by the Lord blessing every endeavor he attempted,[3] God appeared to him, directed him to return to the land of his fathers, and promised His abiding presence with him as he went.[4] Jacob readily admitted that his safety and success had been due to God's presence with him just as He had promised in the dream at least fourteen years earlier.[5] Finally, in a sequel dream God spoke again to Jacob, saying,

> "**I am the God of Bethel**, where you anointed a pillar, where you made a vow to Me; now arise, leave this land, and return to the land of your birth." (Gen. 31:13, emphasis mine)

Jacob returned to Shechem, erected an altar there, and named it El-Elohe-Israel, which means God, the God of Israel.

---

[1] Gen. 28:20-22.
[2] Cf., e.g., Gen. 31:1-21.
[3] Gen. 30:30.
[4] Gen. 31:3.
[5] Gen. 31:5-7.

When we remember that Jacob's name had been changed to Israel, we understand that Jacob was saying that the God with whom he had been dealing throughout his sojourn from the land of his birth and back was his God.[1]

The God of Abraham and Isaac had become the God of Jacob without any reference to or discussion of their initial faith in Him. So we must ask, "Why is that?" The answer seems simple enough: the relationship experienced by faith in God was more important to Moses to pass on to the generations that followed than the explicit content of the faith that these men initially believed or when and under what circumstances they had first believed (if, indeed, there had been a specific point at which they first believed). It is wiser to be content with what Moses did reveal. To surmise what wasn't revealed and then extrapolate from those *assumptions* further conjectures, building *conjectures* upon *conjectures*, is dogmatically dangerous.

Neither Isaac nor Jacob could represent by their actions or attitudes either of the two sons in Jesus' *Parable of the Prodigal Son*. They portray neither the son whose heart was far away from the father nor the son whose priorities took him far away from him. Both Isaac and Jacob, even though they both had their issues, were really good sons. As a result they became models for those that would come after them. But their descendants never persisted in well-doing like Isaac and Jacob did.

Jacob had twelve sons, coming from his two wives and their personal handmaids or servants. He was partial to Joseph and Benjamin because they were his two youngest and because they both came from Rachel, his most beloved wife. Leah was his wife too, but he did not love her as he loved Rachel. And she, of

---

[1] Gen. 33:20.

course, was well aware of that.

How *useful* the sons of Jacob were to God is not a subject the Bible explores thoroughly. Most likely they were like both their father and their grandfather. While very few specifics are known of Isaac's faithful walk and *usefulness* to God, it is a Biblical fact that he had such a walk and was, thereby, very *useful* to God. God did not use only extraordinary leaders to help move the world toward His desired goal for it; He used everyone who walked by faith. It was faith that pleased Him not the innate abilities that He had woven into their human make-up.

Joseph believes in God, becomes a useful son

When Joseph was seventeen years old, he had two dreams. In them God revealed to him cryptically how the relationship between himself, his parents, and his brothers would evolve. According to Joseph's dreams, his family would someday bow down before him. Jacob, Joseph's father, was shocked to hear his dreams. Joseph's brothers, who despised him already due to the favoritism their father showed him, now had another reason to hate him even more.

Consider these facts about this family: 1.) Jacob's two wives were sisters who competed with each other for the affections of their husband; 2.) his wives' two handmaids, who were also mothers of most of Jacob's sons, were involved by necessity in this competition; 3.) ten of the brothers, most of whom came from the unloved wife, Leah, and her handmaid, hated this favored son of their other mother. All this makes one wonder if anyone ever had any peace in that household.

Nine of the ten older brothers finally developed a plan to sell Joseph into slavery. While that sounds cruel, it was a better option than their original intent which was to kill him.

As the story developed down in Egypt, we read repeatedly how God protected and cared for Joseph even though He would not immediately release him from his slavery. When he was purchased by Potiphar, the captain of Pharaoh's bodyguard, from the Ishmaelites, who had bought him from Joseph's nine older brothers, he was put in charge of Potiphar's house. The text clearly establishes God's continuing presence with and care for him:

> "And the Lord was *with* Joseph, *so* he became a successful man." (Gen. 39:2)

Once again God's presence was not an idle presence; He was *with* Joseph *in order to* make him successful. Joseph must have in some clear way given his God all the credit for his success because the text continues with this information:

> "Now his master saw that **the Lord was with him and how the Lord caused all** that he did to prosper in his hand." (Gen. 39:3)

In a polytheistic culture, there had to be some kind of clear communication on the part of Joseph that his God was not like those of the Egyptians. *But the way in which Joseph clarified the identity of his God is left unexplained.* The Bible student knows that some distinction must have been made, but the Bible doesn't explain *explicitly* how it was done.

...

God wants His children to explain His uniqueness
from their own experience of Him.

...

Sometime later, the Pharaoh's cupbearer and baker were incarcerated in the same jail in which Joseph was being held.

(Joseph was in jail due to Potiphar's wife's false accusation of attempted rape.) Eventually they each had a dream, and Joseph offered to interpret their dream for them. But he made it clear to them that the interpretation could be obtained, but it must come from his God. He made this point with a question he asked:

> "Do not interpretations belong to God?" (Gen. 40:8)

The fact that the text does not go into a dialogue about which God Joseph was referring to leads us to assume that Joseph had, again, somehow made it clear to all who knew him that his God was not the same as any of their gods.

Two years later Pharaoh had a dream that troubled him greatly. Joseph was called in to interpret that dream because Pharaoh's cupbearer remembered his ability to obtain interpretations to dreams. But once again Joseph explained that it is his God and not he nor any other man who interprets dreams. He said,

> "It is not in me [to give the interpretation that you seek]; God will give Pharaoh a favorable answer." (Gen. 41:16)

And after the dream was revealed, Joseph said,

> "God has told Pharaoh what He is about to do." (Gen. 41:25, 28)

This short history of Joseph's life illustrates Joseph's faith in the one, true God quite well. While his faith in God is indisputable, once again the Bible does not give the moment when he first began to trust in God or the content that he believed at that time (if there were such a time). The Bible does not use Joseph's continuing faith to prove the genuineness of His faith, but to show how he became a *useful* son who saved the line of Messiah from extinction. Continuing faith cannot prove the genuineness of one's faith any more than continuing recall proves the validity of one's past memories.

Joseph's brothers believe, become useful sons

The severe famine, that had been revealed to Pharaoh in his dreams and accurately interpreted by Joseph, affected not only Egypt but also the land of Canaan where Jacob and his eleven sons and their descendants lived.[1] Eventually Jacob was forced to send ten of his sons, keeping his favorite and the youngest of all at home, to Egypt to purchase the grain that they heard was available there.[2]

When the ten sons of Jacob arrived, Joseph immediately recognized his brothers[3] even after almost twenty years of separation from them. And, interestingly enough, he also remembered the dreams that he had been given of all of his family bowing down before him.[4] Joseph accused his brothers of being spies, presumably, as a ruse to find out whether his father and his brother Benjamin were still alive.[5] He then used this charade to force his brothers to bring Benjamin with them on their next trip. And to insure that they did bring him, he imprisoned Simeon until they returned with Benjamin.[6]

In the midst of their dialogue, Joseph admitted to his brothers, who still did not recognize him, that *he feared God*.[7] That confession must have resonated with his brothers in some meaningful way. He was admitting that he feared *their* God, and

---

[1] Gen. 41:53-57.
[2] Gen. 42:1-5.
[3] Gen. 42:7, 8.
[4] Gen. 42:9.
[5] Gen. 42:13.
[6] Gen. 42:24, 36.
[7] Gen. 42:18.

that fear gave the brothers a little hope of extricating themselves from the danger they were in. So, Simeon was held while they returned home to fetch Benjamin. God used all that happened from this point onward to prick their conscience concerning their past sins against Joseph.

On the way back home, one of the brothers opened his satchel to get some of the grain to feed the donkeys carrying the provisions that they had purchased. When he did, he saw that the money he had paid for the grain was in the sack along with the grain. None of the brothers took the return of their money as a blessing. Rather, all of them turned toward each other and said trembling,

> "What is this that God has done to us?" (Gen. 42:28)

They obviously saw their predicament as the hand of their God *against* them. Such a conviction necessarily leads us to believe that they had a keen sense of accountability before God. How exactly this sense of responsibility developed we are not told. But when we remember that they had no written Scriptures, it is very intriguing that their moral consciousness was so strong.[1] Their guilt was revealed earlier in the text when they stood before Joseph, bemoaning their dilemma, saying,

> "Truly **we are guilty** concerning our brother, because we saw the distress of his soul when he pleaded with us, yet we would not listen; **therefore this distress has come upon us.**" (Gen. 42:21, emphases mine)

---

[1] Of course the same can be said for those who appear outside the lineage of those whom God had chosen to use in a specific way. Abimelech is an example of this person (Gen. 20:1-6). It may be that all this is simply an evidence of the conscience that God instilled in all men when He created them. Or, it could be the result of continuing appearances of the Lord God to His creatures, instilling in them His perspective. If so, then once again, God has not left Himself without a witness.

God had been *with* Joseph. And God had been with his brothers, too! But He was working in their lives very differently.

...

Their evil deed of selling Joseph into slavery nearly twenty years earlier was still plaguing their souls.

...

When they returned home, they relayed to Jacob their father all that had transpired down in Egypt. When another trip to Egypt became unavoidable, Jacob finally relented to send Benjamin with his brothers back to Egypt.

As soon as they arrived in Egypt, they were invited to dine with Joseph. Gripped with fear, they told Joseph's steward about the money found in their sacks and that they wanted to return it. The steward's response offers a clear declaration concerning the spiritual condition of Joseph's brothers. In his reply the steward said,

> "Be at ease, do not be afraid. ***Your God and the God of your father*** has given you treasure in your sacks." (Gen. 43:23, emphases mine)

Before they departed for home at the end of their second trip to Egypt, Joseph ordered his steward to fill his brothers' sacks with food, and return their money to them once again. But he also commanded him to put his silver divination cup in the sack of the youngest brother before they left. After the cup was discovered in Benjamin's sack by Joseph's steward, who had put it there in the first place and who had been sent after them to retrieve it, they all returned to the city to answer to Joseph.

Judah conveyed to Joseph Jacob's reservation in allowing Benjamin to accompany the other brothers to Egypt. The family, he explained, was caught between two dilemmas: everyone was in danger of dying from hunger because of the continuing famine, and Jacob was in danger of dying from grief if anything happened to Benjamin on the trip to Egypt. Judah explained how he had become surety to his father for Benjamin's safe return.[1] It was Judah, you will remember, that decided to sell Joseph to the Ishmaelites in the first place. It was Judah who hated the favoritism shown by Jacob toward both Joseph and Benjamin because they were sons of Jacob's favorite wife, Rachel. But Judah continued to be under great conviction over his past sins.

So, now he was willing to give his own life for one of the brothers that he had so utterly despised earlier in his life. Whether Judah had changed or not, the text doesn't say. But it does lead the reader to know for certain that he deeply loved his father. When Joseph heard Judah's plea to exchange his own life for that of Benjamin's, he broke down in tears and revealed his identity to his brothers.[2]

In the aftermath of this little test by Joseph, God revealed through Jacob and through Joseph enough information to be quite certain about how God viewed the brothers of Joseph. God first revealed His will to Jacob concerning whether or not to believe his sons, upon their return from Egypt, and move to Egypt to live. In doing so, He implied that Jacob's descendants would have *the privilege of God's presence with them in Egypt* and that He would eventually bring them back to the land of Canaan which He had promised to give them as an inheritance. God's revelation to Jacob was clear:

> "I am God, the God of your father [i.e., Isaac]; do not be afraid to go down to Egypt, for *I will make you a great nation there. I will*

---

[1] Gen. 44:18-34.
[2] Gen. 45:1-15.

> *go down with you to Egypt*, and *I will also surely bring you up again*; and Joseph will close your eyes." (Gen. 46:3-4, emphases and bracket mine)

While they grew into a great nation, *God was with them*. And remember that God's presence is never an idle presence.

How exactly He demonstrated His presence we are not told. But as we saw in Joseph's case, when the text says that God is *with* a person, it means that God was there to bless what he undertook as he remained faithful to Him. Since Jacob lived a very short time while in Egypt, God was promising His care and protection to all twelve tribes arising from Jacob's twelve sons who were the heads of those tribes.

Joseph also described his brothers' relationship with God as he reiterated God's promised care of them while they remained in Egypt. He told them:

> "I am about to die, but *God will surely take care of you*, and bring you up from this land to *the land which He promised on oath* to Abraham, to Isaac, and to Jacob." (Gen. 50:24, emphases mine)

So, the God who shepherded Jacob all of his life[1] will be there to care for all of the sons of Jacob and for all of their descendants throughout their sojourn down in Egypt. He will provide for them as He had for their father.

Nowhere is the coming of a Messiah made the focus of anyone's faith at this point in the story of the Bible. Whatever they knew of Him was minimal; whatever they believed about Him was not passed down to us in the infallible record of the Scriptures. It is best then that we focus upon what the Scriptures give us rather than deducing conclusions that are not *forced* upon us.

---

[1] Gen. 48:15-16.

Responding to the one, true God produced *useful* sons. Their belief was in a personal God who was present with them to take care of them. Their responsibility was to respond to this God who was making Himself known. But never is there described a movement from an eternally condemned state to an eternally saved state as our orthodox theologies teach. The issue was whether God's creatures would represent Him well or poorly, whether they would live righteously or wickedly, whether they would live by faith or not. What lifestyle did they choose? It was a winding path to be sure.

Moses raised up as savior

To answer that question more specifically we have to skip forward 400 years. It is now approximately 1525 B.C. It was during this time that the children of Israel became enslaved in Egypt after a new dynasty of Pharaohs came to power.[1] After 400 years would a belief in the one, true God still exist among Jacob's descendants? If it did still exist, would it be sufficient to maintain some sort of bond between the people and their God? After all, He was allowing such suffering in their lives. Would their present suffering quench the faith that once existed in the God of Jacob? Did Jacob's twelve sons, the patriarchs of the twelve tribes, pass on their faith effectively to their descendants?

The drama began as God called Moses, the man who would become Israel's Savior. And what kind of Savior (or deliverer) would he be? The same kind that Israel expected the Messiah to be:[2] a Savior from physical oppression. Will that divine information be wasted on us? Will our theological training transform the Biblical

---

[1] Gen. 15:13-14; Ex. 1:8-11.
[2] Deut. 18:15-20 has been traditionally taken to refer to the Messiah: one like Moses.

perspective of a Savior who delivers man from the trials he faces *on* the earth into a Savior who delivers man *from* the earth?

In the conversation between God and Moses, long before Moses ever got to Egypt, God revealed some pertinent information about the spiritual status of the descendants of Jacob living there. The twelve sons of Jacob (including their descendants after them) are now regularly called "the sons of Israel." That name, Israel, was chosen by God and given to Jacob to memorialize *his tenacity in overcoming men while holding onto God*.[1] As God spoke to Moses from the burning bush, Moses hid his face and heard a thrilling, divine testimony concerning the spiritual state of his Jewish brethren. Moses later recorded this testimony for all the generations that would follow:

> "And the Lord said, 'I have surely seen the affliction of *My people* who are in Egypt, and *have given heed to their cry* because of their taskmasters, for *I have come down to deliver them* from the power of the Egyptians, and to *bring them up from the land to a good land and spacious land*, to a land flowing with milk and honey . . . . Therefore, come now, and I will send you to Pharaoh, so that you may bring *My people, the sons of Israel*, out of Egypt.'" (Ex. 3:7-8, 10, emphases mine)

Before Moses was sent by God to physically deliver Israel from Egyptian slavery, God established the people's spiritual status by calling the whole nation *His people* and *His first-born* as well.[2] God considered the whole congregation of this people as one person; He considered the whole multitude, including men, women, and children, *His first-born son*. If God calls a person His, that person is His. If He calls the whole nation His first-born, they should be thought of in just that way and in no other.

---

[1] Gen. 32:24-28.
[2] Ex. 4:22. Cf. Ex. 4:23.

...
All the people of Israel are declared to be God's sons by God Himself!
...

Looking through the right window never distorts reality. Using the right paradigm brings understanding.

The three signs given to Moses

God gave this hesitant Savior three signs to convince Israel that their God, the God of their forefathers, had sent him. These three signs were meant to bring the whole multitude of the sons of Israel to believe that Moses was ordained by their God to deliver them out of Egypt. It seems apparent that God was telling Moses that *if* Israel could be convinced that the God of Abraham, of Isaac, and of Jacob, and thus their God too, had sent Moses, ***then*** they would accept him as their leader. According to the Scriptures, then, all three signs were given . . .

> "that they may ***believe that the Lord, the God of their fathers ... has appeared to you***. And it shall come about that if they will ***not believe*** you or heed the witness of the first sign (the staff that turns into a snake), they may ***believe*** the witness of the last sign (his hand becoming leprous and returning to normal again). But it shall be that if they will ***not believe*** even these two signs or heed what you say, then you shall take some water from the Nile and pour it on the dry ground; and the water which you take from the Nile will become blood on the dry ground." (Ex. 4:5, 6-9, emphases mine)

This precaution on the part of God in His preparation of Israel's Savior demands that the people were so committed to their God that they wouldn't follow just anyone.

> *The issue was not whether the people were believers in God; the issue was whether the people would follow Moses if he could not prove to them that their God -- the one, true God -- had sent him to them.*

They were going to need proof that their God was involved. Given their circumstances, such a need could have been predicted just as God had done.

When Moses finally arrived in Egypt, he went to the elders of the people to convince them that God had heard their cries and was preparing to *save* them. Then Moses showed the leaders the signs that God had given him. The elders' response? Just what you would expect:

> "He then performed the signs in the sight of the people. *So the people believed*; and when they heard that *the Lord was concerned about the sons of Israel* and that He had seen their affliction, *then they bowed low and worshiped*." (Ex. 4:30-31, emphases mine)

The nation of Israel had not only been believers in the God of their forefathers, but now their faith was invigorated to believe that He was going to deliver them from their bondage. As a result, they worshiped the Lord their God from a heart of thanksgiving and praise.

> *But a strong commitment doesn't always produce a vital faith.*

But there were going to be some obstacles!

In His commission to Moses, God had warned him that Pharaoh would be obstinate and would not let Israel go. So, when he got down to Egypt, Moses was commanded to warn

Pharaoh that if he refused to let the people go, his first-born son would be killed by the God of the Jews. God's directions to Moses were recorded as follows:

> "Then you shall say to Pharaoh, 'Thus says the Lord, *"Israel is My son, My first-born*. So I said to you, 'Let *My son* go, that he may serve Me;' but you have refused to let him go. Behold, I will kill *your son, your first-born*." (Ex. 4:22-23, emphases mine)

This is as intimate a picture of Israel's relationship with her God as can be given in human language. The whole nation of Israel was likened to the son of Pharaoh. Just as Pharaoh had a son, so did God. Just as Pharaoh's son was loved, so was Israel. Just as Pharaoh's son was in line to rule his kingdom, so was Israel (a point to be revealed later by Jesus).[1] We must never lose sight of the fact that God viewed the Israelites in the most intimate terms one can apply to the relationship between God and humans: *they had a Father-son relationship*.

While there were moments of despondency and resistance,[2] they were still God's sons, and He was their Father. Ultimately they did follow Moses, but they never did so with a whole heart.

God had redeemed (or bought) them with an outstretched arm and with great judgments.[3] Consequently, God required every family to "redeem back" or buy back from Him with money every first-born male child.[4] All Israel was included in the first redemption[5] -- because the whole nation was His first-

---

[1] Matt. 25:14-30; Lk. 19:11-27.
[2] E.g., Ex. 9:6.
[3] Ex. 6:6; Deut. 4:34; 26:8. This is not a spiritual redemption in the traditional sense. They already believed in God and were called "sons" by God Himself before they were physically redeemed from the hand of the Egyptians and from the land of Egypt. No spiritual concept to be discerned here at all.
[4] Ex. 12:22-28; 13:11-15.
[5] Ex. 12:3, 6, 27, 41, 42, 47, 50.

born son -- and all Israel commemorated their belief in the God of Israel after their deliverance from Egypt with the yearly feast of Passover and Unleavened Bread.[1]

What an effective way this is to teach succeeding generations that their God is the one, true God to whom the nation owes its existence, and each person owes his life! It makes one wonder whether this is the point of the Lord's Supper as well.

How were the 10 plagues designed to be used?

When trials come, it is natural to debate whether one is walking in the right path or not. What was the people's initial response to Moses when their affliction increased? It was anything but spiritual. But that is exactly how faith operates. One moment it can be *vital*, and the next moment it may be *idle*.

…
The belief that they had so readily expressed earlier was no longer evident in them.
…

They responded much like believers have done through the centuries by praising God when things are going well or when there is hope of good times in the foreseeable future, but complaining and grumbling when they are called upon to endure hardships of any kind. The text describes it this way:

> "So Moses spoke . . . to the sons of Israel [all the promises God gave to Moses for them], but they did not listen to Moses on account of their despondency and cruel bondage." (Ex. 6:9, bracket is a summary of the immediate context)

Those who eventually walked out of Egypt behind Moses

---

[1] Ex. 14:31; 15:13, 16.

were given the command to repeatedly explain to their children and their children's children all that God did in Egypt to save them. The Passover itself was intended to be a perpetual memorial of Israel's physical redemption from Egypt. It was to be a feast, celebrating the miraculous intervention of the God in whom they had believed and by whose hand they had been saved.

Almost the whole nation from this time onward, with the exception of the periodic revivals that were experienced, portrays the two sons in Jesus' *Parable of the Prodigal Son*. They were a believing people who were enticed by the world, the flesh, and the Devil.

...

*Sometimes they were **useful**;*
*at other times they were **useless**.*
*But at all times they were **sons***

...

But God never had the authors of Scripture record the fact that He ceased considering this rebellious, obstinate, hardhearted people *His sons*. This is the demonstrable fact reiterated throughout the entire OT. Only a badly constructed theology can throw Israel under the bus. Unfortunately, such a theology much of Christendom has managed to formulate and maintain for over five hundred years.

This is the reason that nowhere in Israel's history is evangelism (in the traditional sense of that term) ever described or seen as the need of this people or for any other people for that matter. They all were sons by creation, but they have repeatedly gone astray, have repeatedly incurred God's discipline for it, and have repeatedly needed to repent in order to move back into fellowship with the God that they knew. This M.O. is not only true in the OT, it is also true in the Gospels of the NT. This will make a huge difference in the way we interpret those books of the Bible. It will also make a huge difference in how we relate to all the other people of the world. Begin thinking on this now.

Conclusion

> Abraham …
> Isaac …
> Jacob …
> Jacob's twelve sons …
> The descendants of these twelve sons, the nation of Israel …
> All sons of God!

This is both the initial assumption of the text and its verified reality.

The Bible never isolates or emphasizes initial faith as we are taught to do today. We will never correctly grasp the condition of man upon this earth until we are able to explain that omission. We ignore this fact to our own detriment. The OT's M.O. is persistent: *it **never** focuses upon the point a person first believes in God; rather, it assumes that the person, if he is a main character, does believe in God, and then proceeds to describe his walk, or the lack of one, with the God that he knows.* The OT **never** portrays a person becoming a believer as he leaves a state of unbelief behind. But it does describe people who know God but who waver between following Him and following the desires of their own hearts.

When did they first believe? What did they believe?

The answers to these questions are nowhere specified. We must be content with that.[1]

To be a son of God is to be created by God; to be a *useful* son is to have a vital relationship with the God that you know by walking by faith in Him.

---

[1] Deut. 29:29.

Chapter 7

Israel: from the exodus to the exile

"Rise up, get out from among my people, both you and the sons of Israel...," said Pharaoh. The Israelites didn't need to be told twice!

The journey, however, to the Promised Land would be anything but a quick and easy trip! For 40 years, the nation of Israel lived and wandered in the desert. But they did this *with a visible sign of God's presence among them*. A pillar of cloud by day and a pillar of fire by night were placed in the midst of the people to lead the nation and to protect her from enemy nations.

The presence of their God was visible.

He talked to His people.

He guided and protected the obedient and disciplined the disobedient among them.

The God who had just delivered them from bondage by sending ten extraordinary plagues upon the land of Egypt now reassured this same people that He would not forsake them in their journey. Israel's physical redemption has been forever memorialized in the Passover feast that the nation would observe forty times before they ever moved into their own permanent dwellings in the land of promise.

God knew His people; and they certainly knew Him.

Until my last edit of this manuscript, this chapter was twenty-five pages long, in its shortest form. I have decided that the case against initial faith and the traditional understanding of justification has been effectively made. So I will summarize the Bible's confirmation that the nation of Israel (representing all the people groups of the world by application) knew God and was responding to Him, albeit very poorly at times. There was *never* a need for evangelism (as we understand that term today) to take place. There was need of repentance and receptivity to God's continuing revelation. In short, they were *never* in need of *conversion*. They were in need of *illumination*. God would be in charge of the convicting work, making sure it was effective.

For convenience sake I will break down Israel's history leading up to the time of Christ into three large sections: 1.) their spiritual state during and after their wilderness wanderings; 2.) their spiritual state after entering the Promised Land and while they were united under one king; 3.) their spiritual state from the time of their division into two separate kingdoms to the time of Christ. Using the explicit statements of the Bible alone, the conclusions reached below ought to be sound and authoritative.

The wilderness generations

When Moses instructed the new generation, that had succeeded the 600,000 to 1,200,000 (at least) that had died off in the wilderness wanderings, he said to them,

> "These forty years *the Lord your God has been with you*; you have not lacked a thing." (Deut. 2:7, emphasis mine)

and

> "*Your eyes have seen* all that *the Lord your God* has done to these two kings [Og, king of Bashan and Sihon, king of Heshbon]; so the Lord shall do to all the kingdoms into which you are about to cross. Do not fear them, for *the Lord your God is the one fighting for you*." (Deut. 3:21-22, emphases and bracket mine)

What God did for the first generation, He did for the second generation. Consequently, He commanded them to pass on their faith to their children and to their grandchildren. And it should be noted that this command is given in a context that suggests that Israel's succeeding generations might possibly apostatize from God if they weren't trained well.

...

Not everyone who knows God perseveres in his faith.

...

Moses warned the people about the possibility of apostasy with these words:

> "Only give heed to yourself and keep your soul diligently, ***lest you forget*** the things which your eyes have seen, and ***lest they depart from your heart all the days of your life; but make them known to your sons and your grandsons***." (Deut. 4:9, emphases mine)

Apostasy, becoming a prodigal son or daughter, has always been a possibility for every person God has created. And sadly, apostasy has been the actual experience of a great many in every generation who were formerly faithful to God. The first generation of Israelites which stood before the Lord at Mt. Horeb (Sinai) was instructed to

> "learn the fear of the Lord all the days [you] live on the earth and teach [your] children" this same fear.[1]

Spiritual training takes on a dramatic intensity when you know with absolute certainty that you are on a 38-year death march because of your disobedience. Every adult would die, leaving only those who were twenty years old and younger.

---

[1] Deut. 4:10, the second personal pronoun has been inserted for the third person plural to smooth out the reading.

Just before the nation invades the Promised Land, Moses prepped them by saying,

> "Now this is the commandment, the statutes and the judgments which ***the Lord your God*** has commanded me to teach you, that you might do them in the land where you are going over to possess it, ***so that you and your son and your grandson might fear the Lord your God, to keep His statutes and His commandments***, which I command you all the days of your life, and that your days might be prolonged." (Deut. 6:1-2, emphases mine)

Did you notice that the presumption of the Lord is that at least the first two generations that were to follow would believe in Him and follow Him? Yet that presumption does not include the assumption that any of the generations that followed, including the first two, had to persevere in their faith.

Consequently, right after giving Israel the instructions summarized in Deut. 6:1-2, Moses gave them this warning:

> "... [basically, after the Lord has made you wealthy], then watch yourself, ***lest you forget the Lord*** who brought you from the land of Egypt, out of the house of slavery. You shall ***fear only the Lord your God; and you shall worship Him***, and swear by His name. ***You shall not follow other gods***, any of the gods of the peoples who surround you, for ***the Lord your God in the midst of you*** is a jealous God; otherwise the anger of ***the Lord your God*** will be kindled against you, and He will wipe you off the face of the earth (or land)." (Deut. 6:12-15, emphases mine)

The second generation knew, feared, and worshipped the one, true God. They were His people; and He was their God. Yet problems still existed in the spiritual lives of this generation.

...

Faith in and worship of the one, true God may be accompanied by faith in and worship of false gods.

...

Apparently, throughout the entire 40 years of wandering, while they worshipped and served the Lord, they were not single minded in it. Joshua 24:14-15 tell us that they continued to worship idols even as they worshipped God.[1] So God admonished His people with these words:

> "Now, therefore, fear the Lord and serve Him in sincerity and truth; and *put way the gods which your fathers served beyond the River and in Egypt*, and serve the Lord. And *if it is disagreeable in your sight to serve the Lord*, choose for yourselves today whom you will serve: whether *the gods which your fathers served* which were beyond the River, *or the gods of the Amorites* in whose land you are living; but as for me and my house, we will serve the Lord." (Joshua 24:14-15, emphases mine)

Apparently, both the first generation and the second generation continued to be idolaters even while they worshipped and served the one, true God. And it is note worthy that God left the matter in their hands for them to make the choice concerning whom they would actually serve going forth. But whether they were idol worshippers or not, they never ceased to be God's sons. Prodigals make such compromises that a wholly devoted heart to God no longer exists within them. Yet, God loves them still.

While the nation would eventually make their way into the Promised Land … the seeds of compromise existed within their hearts naturally and would continually manifest themselves as they attempted to conquer the land given to them by God..

Israel: in the land and united

Skip forward about three hundred years …

After enduring the reigns of various judges divinely raised

---

[1] Cf., also, 2Kgs 18:3-4.

up to save particular tribes, sometimes contemporaneously, from the hardships they had brought upon themselves as they wandered away from God, the people finally cried out to God for a monarchal system of government. They wanted a king to reign over them like all the surrounding nations had.

When God spoke to the prophet Samuel on this matter, He revealed the underlying reason for their request for a king. What God revealed about His people ought to establish the truth once and for all that a believer, as defined by Heb. 11:6, may never look like what we are told today all believers must look like if they are *true sons* of God. And the description that God gave here is plainly repeated many times in the Scriptures:

> "And the Lord said to Samuel, 'Listen to the voice of the people in regard to all that they say to you, for they have not rejected you, but ***they have rejected Me from being king over them.*** Like all the deeds which they have done ***since the day that I brought them up from Egypt even to this day -- in that they have forsaken Me and served other gods --*** so they are doing to you also.'" (1Sam. 8:7-8, emphases mine)

After living in the Promised Land, a land flowing with milk and honey, for over three hundred years, those who believed in the God of Israel were still double-minded: they believed in the one, true God, but they also served and worshipped other gods as well.

The people believed in God but they didn't want Him to rule over them completely.

...

They believed in God, but they continued to manifest most of the vices that God's Law condemned.

...

They believed in the one, true God, but they didn't want to

serve Him as some of their forefathers had done. *Nevertheless, God would continue to own them as His own people without hesitation.*

While the three great kings of Israel, Saul, David, and Solomon, epitomized the glory years of the nation, the spiritual state of its people *never* became what God desired. Even though their moral and spiritual corruption was the subject matter of the prophets that God sent to them, their status as God's chosen people was never questioned. In fact, all the prophets resoundingly made it clear that *the people whom they addressed were God's people, and God Himself owned them as such throughout their whole history.* When God Himself declares what is true, shouldn't that settle the matter? God's people never need to be evangelized in our contemporary use of that term.

Israel: one nation, two kingdoms

To obtain an accurate picture of the spiritual condition of the nation of Israel, now divided into two kingdoms, a Northern Kingdom called *Israel* and a Southern Kingdom called *Judah*, one needs only to look into the ministries and messages of the prophets God sent to both kingdoms. And while this should not be overly stressed, the two kingdoms resemble at times the two sons in Jesus' *Parable of the Prodigal Son.*

...

God deals with one people although they now consist of two kingdoms.

...

Although the Northern Kingdom is more egregious in its rebellion against God than is the Southern Kingdom, both are dealt with as God's people and as His *sons who are not only accountable to Him but who are expected to walk by faith in Him.* The prophets will confirm Israel's continuing special status before God as His chosen instrument even while its people adamantly cling to its corrupt moral and spiritual behavior.

...

When one's walk does not match his relationship, he is said to not be the son he ought to be.

...

The prophet Hosea named his third child Lo-ammi which means "not My people." This name refers to Israel's spiritual condition that brought upon its people God's judgment. In this context, "not being God's people" was a reference to their unfaithful walk. God would be their God, and they would be His people *if they walked a certain way, namely, according to all of His laws and precepts.*[1]

From the time of their organization as a kingdom, before the kingdom became divided into northern and southern divisions or sub-kingdoms, their walk was never what it should have been. Finally, God judged them for it. He waited over 200 years hoping they would repent and turn back to Him. He is waiting today for the same reason: not for people to begin a relationship with Him, but for those who have a relationship with Him to walk consistently as they ought to walk.[2]

God continued to love Israel even though she turned her back on Him to love other gods. But while Israel became faithless and set aside her love for God, He continued to love her and has promised to love her steadfastly forever. She may not be faithful, but He will be, loving her with a love that will eventually "heal her apostasy"[3] and bring her to repentance[4]

---

[1] E.g., Ex. 19:5-6; Jer. 7:23; 11:3-4, 5.
[2] 2Pet. 3:1,9. Carefully from the context determine the identity of the "you."

and back to faithfulness.

...

*Their sonship was in place through creation;
it was their fellowship that God sought.*

...

The spiritual state of the nation of Israel is conclusively identified when God Himself declared through the prophet Hosea that

He **"had been the Lord [her] God since [her exodus from] the land of Egypt."**[1]

That is a definitive statement which should settle the debate over Israel's spiritual state for the last six hundred years! From the time of the Exodus and the giving of the Law all the way to the ninth century prophets, God declares through Hosea that Israel had been *His people*. That is the reason there is no evangelism seen in the OT over this period of time. You don't evangelize (in the contemporary sense of that term) those who already know God. Those you lead to a deeper communion.

Though Israel was His people, God was sending Assyria to conquer them as judgment upon their rebellion and apostasy. On the authority of God's word then, Israel was never a spiritually lost and eternally condemned people, needing to be initially saved by God so that her people could become *sons*. From the time she came out of bondage in Egypt to the time of Hosea the prophet, the one, true God was always *her* God.

As Hosea wrote primarily about Israel, the Northern Kingdom, Isaiah wrote primarily about Judah, the Southern

---

[3] Hos. 14:4.
[4] Cf., Rom. 2:4.
[1] Hos. 12:9; 13:4.

Kingdom and Jerusalem, its capital, around 739 B.C. even though he also recorded God's warnings of judgment against Babylon, Assyria, Egypt, and Israel, the Northern Kingdom. The book is filled with Messianic prophecies to help identify Him when He came. Several elements of the work that the Messiah had to accomplish are outlined, and the kingdom that He would eventually establish is described. So, for example, Isaiah predicted the Messiah's virgin birth,[1] His lineage, and righteous rule -- when His kingdom is established[2] -- and His propitiatory death.[3]

While Isaiah is sometimes called the evangelistic book of the Old Testament, it is not about saving the eternally condemned unbeliever. It is about warning those who are already God's people that judgment was coming upon them unless they repented and turned back to Him.

Isaiah was sufficiently clear throughout the entirety of his book that he had in mind people who knew God. In God's own words, they ought to be described this way:

> Isa. 1:2: "*Sons* I have reared up and brought up, but they *have revolted against Me*." (emphasis mine)

God referred to the nation as *sons* that He had raised up. He didn't say that Israel *looked like* sons or *acted like* sons when, in fact, they weren't sons. He said they were indeed His sons! Yet they had rebelled against Him.

It is not the lack of clarity that keeps some from accepting God's words here. It is the fact that they are looking through a poorly made windowpane that is distorting the image upon

---

[1] Isa. 7:14.
[2] Isa. 2:1-11; 9:1-7; 11:1−12:6; 24:1−27:13; 59:1−66:24.
[3] Isa. 52:13−53:12.

which they are gazing. Their windowpane, or theological grid, won't let the text speak for itself. Does yours?

After describing the Southern Kingdom as His sons who are rebelling against Him, God then contrasted their inordinate wandering to the natural instincts of animals:

> Isa. 1:3: "An ox knows its owner, And a donkey its master's manger, But Israel does not know, **My people do not understand**."

God says that *His people* don't have the sense that beasts of burden have instinctively. They were slower than an ox and dumber than a jackass, morally and spiritually speaking. In the NT,[1] God refers to those who know Him in similar ways to emphasize the facts that they don't naturally receive His truth nor do they naturally change their own lifestyle. God's people can walk righteously or wickedly; they can believe or refuse to believe. *The issue in the Bible is between being independent or being dependent, not between being moral and Christian versus being immoral and unchristian.* God is seeking those who will walk in such a way that they depend upon Him in everything for everything.

...

An independent, moral life is just as sinful as a rebellious, immoral life.

...

Israel's sinful desertion from God was described by Isaiah in this very descriptive and definitive way:

> Isa.1:4: "Alas, sinful nation, People weighed down with iniquity, Offspring of evildoers, **Sons who act corruptly**! They have **abandoned** the Lord, They have **despised** the Holy One of Israel, They have **turned away** from Him." (emphases mine)

---

[1] Cf., Matt. 7:6; 2Pet. 2:18-22.

God's description of His own chosen people as a *sinful* nation which was weighed down with *iniquity* doesn't sound like the necessary, radical change in a true believer's life that we have been taught to expect, does it? Rather, God's *sons acted corruptly*; they not only *abandoned* Him, they also *despised* Him. Ask yourself, "How can a person who acts corruptly, abandons, and despises God actually be a son who resembles the Father?"

Without belaboring the point any further,[1] let me use a couple of passages to describe the thesis that is being suggested for the overall message the Bible is communicating. Writing around 640-620 B.C., Zephaniah basically described for his readers Israel's perennial, spiritual problem when he said,

> "Woe to her who is rebellious and defiled, the tyrannical city! She heeded no voice; She accepted no instruction. She did *not trust in the Lord*; She did *not draw near* to her God." (Zeph. 3:1-2, emphases mine)

Jerusalem, the capital of the Southern Kingdom, housed a people that would not receive advice from God or from His prophets; they would not trust daily in the Lord to meet their needs even though they had walked with Him on and off in the past as His *sons*. To use the language of Zephaniah, *their spiritual condition kept them from drawing near to the Lord, their God*. They knew the one, true God and had trusted Him in many ways. Consequently, He is described as *their* God.

But they were not drawing near to Him even though they had relied upon Him at different times in their past. To not draw near to God is simply another way of saying that they refused to walk with Him; they refused to obey Him.

---

[1] Yet the reader ought to at least ponder the following verses which affirm the points being made here: Isa. 44:17-19; 49:26; 63:8-10, 11, 14, 19; 64:5-9.

...
The people of Israel believed in God, but they were not changed into better people by that belief.
...

Each man's own tyrannical heart was the problem, a problem that still exists in every person today. Change could come only from walking in dependence upon God, the same as it does today.

...
According to Haggai, Israel's spiritual condition had not changed over the passage of time.
...

Skipping to near the end of the OT, Haggai made a significant reference to the nation that God had brought out of Egypt. From generation to generation her spiritual heritage had been passed down. God had promised to make Israel into a kingdom of priests and a holy nation if they followed Him faithfully. The fulfillment of that promise is yet future, but God's presence in the midst of Israel was assured until it happened.

If we go back to the *Book of Exodus* we can get a handle on what God had promised Israel:

> "You . . . have seen what I did to the Egyptians, and how I bore you on eagles' wings, and **brought you to Myself**. Now then, *if* you will indeed obey My voice and keep My covenant, **then you will be** My own possession among all the peoples, for all the earth is Mine; and **you shall be to Me a kingdom of priests and a holy nation**." (Ex. 19:4-6)

> "And **I will dwell among the sons of Israel and will be their God**. And **they shall know** that I am **the Lord their God** who brought them out of the land of Egypt, that I might dwell among them; I

am the Lord *their* God." (Ex. 29:45-46)

"Then Moses said to the Lord, 'See, Thou dost say to me, "Bring up this people!" But Thou Thyself hast not let me know whom Thou wilt send with me. Moreover, Thou hast said, "I have known you by name, and you have also found favor in My sight." Now therefore, I pray Thee, if I have found favor in Thy sight, let me know Thy ways, that I may know Thee, so that I may find favor in Thy sight. Consider too, that *this nation is Thy people*.' And He said, '*My presence shall go with you*, and I will give you rest.' Then he said to Him, '*If Thy presence does not go with us, do not lead us up from here*. For how then can it be known that I have found favor in Thy sight, I and Thy people? *Is it not by Thy going with us, so that we, I and Thy people, may be distinguished from all the other people who are upon the face of the earth?*'" (Ex. 33:12-16)

"And Moses made haste to bow low toward the earth and worship. And he said, 'If now I have found favor in They sight, *O Lord, I pray, let the Lord go along in our midst*, even though *the people are so obstinate*; and do Thou pardon our iniquity and our sin, and take us as Thine own possession.'" (Ex. 34:8-9)

Is it not clear from these passages that God had promised Moses that He would be in the midst of Israel as they came out of Egypt? And when Haggai recorded God's reassurance of His continuing, abiding presence after nine hundred years, does it not seem natural to believe that God had never rejected Israel even after all of her sins and waywardness? This is exactly what God reminded the people of around 520 B.C. through Haggai:

"As for the promise which I made you when you came out of Egypt, *My Spirit is abiding in your midst*; do not fear!" (Hag. 2:5)

Even Israel's obstinate disobedience did not remove its people from being God's chosen servants among whom He promised to abide continually. Israel would always be, from her inception as a nation to her ultimate spiritual cleansing in the coming Great Tribulation, a people who believed in God but who would not depend upon Him wholeheartedly as they should. That was Israel's perpetual problem.

Early in Israel's history, God summarized mankind's basic problem in a question that He asked Moses about Israel:

> "How long will they **not believe in Me**, despite all the signs which I have performed in their midst?" (Num. 14:11)

This is the problem that the whole Bible is given to solve: *how long will it take for a believing people to consistently walk by faith*? Exactly what does it take to achieve this end? That is the problem the Bible is solving. From cover to cover the Bible is explaining how God, in His immense lovingkindness, is trying to lead those who believe in Him to walk consistently by faith.

Every prodigal, if he steps back and takes his eyes off all the barriers that the world, the flesh and the Devil have placed in front of him, can identify examples of God's lovingkindness, grace, mercy, and care extended to him. Regardless of what you have done, regardless of how long you've done it, your heavenly Father is waiting for you to come home.

…
Being a prodigal is natural,
and maintaining that lifestyle also seems natural.
…

The guilt of past sins, the shame of what has been done, and the sense of unworthiness to come to God are persuasive in holding you back. But the fact remains: God loves you, has provided forgiveness for all you've done, and a spiritual life that you've never experienced. Come home.

Chapter 8

The Testimony of Hebrews 11

The eleventh chapter in the *Book of Hebrews* has been called the hall of fame of faith. It begins with a definition of faith in verse one; then it gives in verse two its main theme. From there it gives examples that illustrate the definition of faith in the lives of OT saints. So what is faith? The author is definitive in this matter when he says,

> "Now faith is the **substance** of things hoped for, the **conviction** of things not seen." (Heb. 11:1, author's translation and emphases)

This verse sets forth the essence of faith; it tells us what faith is, no less, but certainly not anything more. Whatever the term translated *substance* by the NKJV or *assurance* by the NASB means, it is synonymous with the concept of *conviction*. Or, more grammatically stated: *substance* (or assurance) is treated as an apposition to the term translated *conviction*. The immediate context will elucidate the meaning of faith so that we can be assured that we fully understand it.

The concept of having or developing a conviction is an easy one. Every *persuasion* that comes from the Bible is the faith God desires in us.

…
Every Biblical conviction is Biblical faith.
…

And every conviction or persuasion is the *substance* to which the author of *the Book of Hebrews* referred. Faith increases as convictions increase. The strength of any particular conviction is not the issue. Each conviction is sufficient for God to bless.

Biblical faith is man's response to what God is saying to him. Hence, the content of faith does not originate within man. Man does not determine what things he is responsible to believe. God tells man the content that he is supposed to believe and the blessings he should seek. By faith or in faith man receives what God is saying to him as true and, if acts are required, he pursues the accomplishment of that divine will as he relies upon God (in the OT) or as he lives by the life that the Spirit instills as he walks by faith (in the NT).

As you read the seventeen specific references in Hebrews chapter eleven to the faith responses given by the men of old, several facts are clear. First, none of these references deal with a person's initial trust in God. Obviously, then, the divine acceptance by God that is *supposedly* needed and that *supposedly* results from an initial belief in the God of Israel is never broached in this chapter just as it is never broached anywhere else in the entire Bible.

…
*Initial faith in God is not only **unimportant**,*
*since the Bible **never** mentions it,*
*it must be quite **irrelevant** to every other doctrine in the Scriptures.*
…

The subject on the mind of the original author is walking by faith or responding to God by faith, but not coming to God initially in faith. This is always the focus of the Bible. Never is the focus on a presumed, but undiscoverable, initial faith.

Second, there is no indication that assurance, in the purely subjective sense of being assured of something, is the author's point or is ever on the mind of the author. Rather the essence of the faith described throughout the chapter is very objective.

...

In each case in Heb.11,
God reveals something of His will to a person,
and that person is responsible
to believe what God has said
and to respond accordingly.

...

So, for example, God warned Noah about the coming flood and commanded him to build an ark. Note how the author of Hebrews explained it:

> "***By faith Noah***, being warned by God about ***things not yet seen***, in reverence ***prepared an ark*** for the ***salvation*** of his household, by which he condemned the world, and became ***an heir by the righteousness which is according to faith***." (Heb. 11:7, emphases mine)

By faith Noah built the ark. That means Noah believed God's warning and built a boat to save himself and his family (along with the animals of course). The salvation that God is speaking about here is a deliverance from the personal destruction that the flood would surely bring. This salvation is obviously distinct from Noah's relationship with God who had already declared that Noah was a righteous man who was blameless in his life ***before*** He ever commissioned him to build an ark.[1]

The detailed picture of this simple command to build an ark would have looked like this: while he built the ark, his

---

[1] Gen. 6:9

motivations of reverence and obedience toward God, the specific task of building the ark, including all the complications and trials along the way, and the purpose for building the ark undergird his life, set the direction his life took, and formed the priorities to which he adhered for one hundred years. In this way he found approval with God! That was Noah's faith.

...

*The content of Noah's faith came from God,
but the corresponding dependence upon God came from Noah.*

...

If Noah had possessed a dead faith, he would have died in the flood along with all the others. And he would have died even though he had been previously singled out by God as a righteous, blameless man. The righteousness that God was seeking in the lives of those whom He intended to save from the flood was a practical righteousness for the Bible knows of no other kind.

Do you not see that walking by faith is not an ethereal approach to life without any substance? While one may be tempted to think of trusting God or of walking by faith as similar to eating cotton candy, it isn't. **Developing faith** *occurs when God's word is assimilated;* **walking by faith** *occurs when those convictions assimilated from God's revelation of His will give direction, meaning, and purpose to a person's life.* Faith then is the substance or conviction formed from God's revelation before that revelation (i.e., the content believed) actually makes a footprint in life through the actions taken. If the faith is *vital*, then the footprints will necessarily be seen. But faith can be present without its telltale footprint because it may be an idle faith instead of an active one.

Third, no one has to be a seminary graduate or a theologian to be a man or woman of faith because faith is simple. It develops within the soul of man whenever he receives God's revelation on any particular issue. How much doctrine must be assimilated, systematized, and regurgitated for genuine faith to be present? The author of Hebrews, following the rest of the authors of Scripture, believed that God is the one responsible for setting that standard, rather than the trained theologians among His people. The author said,

> "And without faith it is impossible to please Him, for he who comes to God must believe *that* He is, *and that* He is a rewarder of those who seek Him." (Heb. 11:6, emphases mine)

For faith to be present a person must believe that God exists. How simple! God is there, and He has revealed Himself to every man coming into the world.[1] Whatever that information is, according to this verse, it appears that it must be minimal instead of the theological list formulated by many of our theologians. Nowhere, that I am aware of, is there any list to be found anywhere in Scripture itemizing what a man must believe to be initially accepted by God, *assuming the indefensible position* that there is such an initial acceptance with God in the first place.

I am suggesting that every person coming into the world has had the same standard: *he had to believe that the only true God was there, and that He would reward each person who responded to the revelation that He was giving him.* The reward is not a heaven-hell issue as many suppose. This is proven by the fact that there is not a single word about either place, heaven or hell, in any of the

---

[1] Ps. 19:1-6; John 1:9; Rom. 1:18-20; Acts 14:16-17; 17:22-31.

seventeen references to faith used by the author of *Hebrews*. So that can't be the reward the author has in mind.

Fourth, the result of believing the revelation that God gave to the men in the OT was that they found *approval* from God. It doesn't say or imply anywhere in the chapter that a person was forgiven of his sins or that he became a member of some undefined community of faith. It only says that by faith "men of old gained approval." To gain approval is to be pleasing to God[1] and to be well spoken of by others when they testified about them.[2]

While the author of the *Book of Hebrews* lists several individuals whose lives at some point gained approval by God, the majority of the people in the OT responded very differently. The very popular, OT verse, that is mostly taken out of context and applied to the United States of America, indicates that God's people can be very dull spiritually:

> "*If* I shut up the heavens so that there is no rain, *or if* I command the locust to devour the land, *or if* I send pestilence among *My people*, and *My people* who are called by My name humble themselves and pray, and seek My face and *turn from their wicked ways, then* I will hear from heaven, will *forgive their sin*, and will heal their land." (2Chron. 7:13-14, emphases mine)

While Hosea stated the problem as God's people having no knowledge:

> "*My people* are destroyed for *lack of knowledge*. Because you have *rejected knowledge*, I also will reject you from being My priest. Since you have *forgotten the law of your God*, I also will forget your children." (Hos. 4:6, emphases mine)

---

[1] Heb. 11:6.
[2] The verb translated "gained approval" in Heb. 11:2, 4, 39 is μαρτυρεω which means to bear witness, to give a good report, or to approve. See G. Abbott-Smith, *A Manuel Greek Lexicon of the New Testament*, T.&T. Clark, Edinburgh, third edition, 1973; pp. 278-79.

Isaiah explained the problem in relation to their sins:

> "Behold, the Lord's hand is not so short That it cannot save; Neither is His ear so dull That it cannot hear. But *your iniquities* have made a separation between you and your God, And *your sins* have hidden His face from you, so that He does not hear." (Isa. 59:1-2, emphases mine)

Unlike those positive examples listed in the eleventh chapter of the book of Hebrews, most of the OT is filled with examples of God's people provoking God to anger by their wicked lifestyles. The Israelites, the divinely chosen people of God, struggled in their pursuit of God. Consistently their spiritual walk with God was of the kind that aroused His anger rather than His pleasure. *Though they believed in God, they hardly lived a life that He could justify.* These two things – knowing God (and believing one is accountable to Him) and living a life that He can justify - are not mutually inclusive. It simply isn't possible to read the Bible without a theological bias and believe otherwise. Try it and you'll see. True faith doesn't always result in genuine godliness.

When we understand that the Bible is about walking by faith, and not coming to God initially in faith, we will be surprised at how simple its story really is. Basically, God promises to accept and bless the person who lives by faith. On the flip side of that coin lies another promise: an independent life, regardless of how moral or how religious it might be, will not be accepted or blessed with God's fellowship, answers to prayer, and personal fulfillment, to mention just a few, random blessings that are usually important to most people.

When we live independent lives, we may be like either one of the two sons in Jesus' *Parable of the Prodigal Son*. While both had the opportunity of having and maintaining a wonderful relationship with their father, they chose not to do so for different reasons. The end result in both cases was missed blessings and, more importantly, missed intimacy with their father. A life of faith pleases God and meets His standard for living. He will *justify* every single response we perform in faith and *condemn* every response performed without faith.

It follows from what I've just said that it is vastly important for every person, Christian and non-Christian alike, to learn how to respond to the one, true God in faith. If your particular local church or organization has not taught you how to walk by faith by now, it is probably time for you to look outside of that community for better instruction on this issue. God is pleased and you are blessed by this kind of lifestyle alone. Don't miss it.

Chapter 9

Jewish Belief at the Time of Christ

If the people living at the time of Christ in the first century believed something that proved to be incorrect about the coming Messiah, did that error in thinking invalidate their faith in the coming Messiah?

Do you think that everyone living at that time and believing in a coming Messiah was on the same page concerning God's promised deliverer?

If those living in the first century and believing in a coming Messiah rejected Jesus as the promised Messiah, did that refusal to believe in Jesus nullify their belief in the God of Israel and in the coming of His promised Messiah?

We are going to take a fresh, independent look at a few of the persons that cross Jesus' path in the NT with particular focus upon some of those mentioned by the apostle John in his Gospel. Surely these individuals can represent "the typical man on the street" in the first century.

…

*In the Gospels we are face to face with persons who had "gained approval" by their faith just as those recorded in Heb. 11 had done, but who were, nevertheless, in need of **saving**!*

…

My premise is a simple one: when we look at these individuals, we find persons who represented Abraham's faith.

He most assuredly was their father in the faith just as he was for those recorded in the pages of the OT. And if we encounter men and women who believed in the God of Israel, what should we conclude about their spiritual condition? Some of the persons we will investigate are *explicitly* described as individuals who believed in the God of Israel; others, we are *explicitly* told, not only believed in Him but also believed that He was sending a Messiah to Israel to be her Savior; and of others these beliefs are certainly implied very strongly, so strongly in fact that they can't be denied except upon some preconceived bias.

The question that arises for all interpreters is an intriguing one: *if these individuals already believed in God, how can John's Gospel be evangelistic in the traditional sense of that concept?*

We need to begin thinking outside the theological box in which we have been packaged. Our programming doesn't seem to fit the historical, cultural milieu of the first century, and that is part of the reason the Bible seems more than a little confusing to us. We've missed its emphasis; we've missed its message.

...

It is unnatural to view the individuals set before us in the Gospel of John as anything other than those who were responding positively, though not completely, to the God of Israel.

...

If the men and women Jesus addressed in His public ministry were following in Abraham's footsteps of faith, they were already pleasing to God and were already being *justified* by Him in the same way Abraham had been. If they were fulfilling the requirements of Heb. 11:6, then they were already living a divinely *approved life* **before** Jesus the Messiah ever began His ministry to them.

This fact then forces the reader to conclude that Jesus must have been offering something that they didn't already possess. Since they were *pleasing to God by the faith* they exercised, as Abraham had been before them and as all of those mentioned in Hebrews chapter eleven had been as well, Jesus couldn't have been offering an initial relationship with God to people who were already walking with God. What, then, was Jesus offering them? Intrigued?

Nicodemus, *a* Pharisee & *the* teacher of the Jews

When we meet Nicodemus in the third chapter of the *Gospel of John*, we learn right away that he is a Pharisee and a ruler of the Jews. The mention of his being a ruler probably refers to the fact that he was a member of the Sanhedrin, the governing body for Israel's religious and social life. Nicodemus was also a teacher. Jesus called Nicodemus *the* teacher of Israel[1] without giving any reason in the immediate context for dismissing or even minimizing that description. As a superior teacher of the OT Scriptures, he must have been well respected and influential in guiding the people and even his peers at the time of Christ.

Being a Pharisee and a member of the Sanhedrin, Nicodemus would have clung to the *Shema* not only as Israel's motto but also as his own personal conviction. This prayer was recited every morning and every evening and got its name from the Hebrew command: Shema Yisra'el (Hear, Israel!). The whole recited prayer comes from Deut. 6:4-9:

> "Hear, O Israel! ***The Lord is our God***, the Lord is one! And you shall love ***the Lord your God*** with all your heart and with all your

---

[1] John 3:10.

soul and with all your might. And these words, which I am commanding you today shall be on your heart; and you shall teach them diligently to your sons and shall talk of them when you sit in your house and when you walk by the way and when you lie down and when you rise up. And you shall bind them as a sign on your hand and they shall be as frontals on your forehead. And you shall write them on the doorposts of your house and on your gates." (Emphases mine)

The *Shema* is not commanding a person to believe in the one, true God; it is commanding a person to love Him throughout the whole day with his whole heart. It is a love for God that the Bible is all about according to Jesus[1] as well as Paul[2] who was a Pharisee himself.[3] Why is love so central? It is central because from love flows the obedience that God seeks.[4]

As Jesus taught His followers to do, we must analyze Nicodemus' words to discern what convictions filled his heart. We ought to consider, more seriously than we typically do, the truth that a confession is a better guide to a person's spiritual convictions than his lifestyle may be. Jesus affirmed this truth when He said,

"the mouth speaks out of that which fills the heart." (Matt. 12:34)

Words spoken in dialogue upon any topic at all are similar to a confession since a man's convictions are revealed in the discussion. This truth, of course, is not to be taken superficially. The confession that a person gives ought to promote the kind of discussion that is able to affirm that he has an accurate understanding of the words that he uses. No one should be content with another person's memorized response learned by

---

[1] Cf., e.g., Matt. 22:34-40.
[2] Cf., e.g., 1Tim. 1:5.
[3] Phil. 3:5
[4] John 14:21, 23.

rote. Jesus emphasized the importance of a person's verbally expressed convictions when He said,

> "For **by your words** you shall **be justified** [in the sense of being approved], and **by your words** you shall be condemned [in the sense of being rejected or not being approved]." (Matt. 12:37, emphases and brackets mine)

We ought to conclude that Nicodemus' comments in the darkness of night shed a great deal of light upon the convictions of his heart. He said,

> "Rabbi, **we know** that **You have come from God** as a teacher; for no one can do these signs that You do unless **God is with him**." (John 3:2, emphases mine)

First, Nicodemus was not only coming for his own enlightenment, he came as a representative of others. Who they were we don't know. But we do know that there were others of like conviction to that of Nicodemus since he said, "**We** know" this about You.

Now it is an extraordinary thing to know, that is, to be sure, that another has come from God. And yet, that is what Nicodemus believed because he confessed to it by his words. And, his assurance is founded upon the very thing that Jesus, and the Father who sent Him, wanted it to be built upon. What was that thing?

Nicodemus' assurance was based upon the miraculous deeds that Jesus was performing. (For an expansion of this thought see points three and four below.) To believe that Jesus was the Messiah because of the works that He was doing was a good thing. God had given Jesus His miracles just as God had given Moses his. In both cases, they were to convince others of the fact that God the Father was behind the ministry that they were observing. And in neither case was the agent that God had sent trying to start a new religion or a new faith. Both Moses and Jesus were pointing their audiences back to the one, true God and to Him alone.

Second, Nicodemus believed in the God of Israel, the God who does mighty deeds as the psalmist described Him.[1] Even Mary the mother of Jesus, who would not have been trained in the Scriptures as a man would have been, and even much less than a Pharisee would have been, described God over thirty years before as the Mighty One who has done great things for her.[2] To affirm that Jesus came from God but not believe that *that God*, who had sent Him, exists is a *non-sequitur*.

...

Bad theology will not keep a person out of heaven,
but it may hinder, or prevent entirely,
his spiritual growth which is all important to God.

...

God is not waiting for the unbeliever to become a conservative theologian before his life can be pleasing to Him. He is waiting for a person to respond to the revelation (either written, personal, or in creation) with which He is convicting him. When he believes that revelation, he is instantly pleasing to and approved by the one, true God who gave him the revelation.

Third, Nicodemus was admitting that Jesus was performing miraculous deeds that could not be attributed to the ability of a human. These mighty deeds originated from God. Nicodemus, as a Jew of the first century, believed that there was only one,

---

[1] Psa. 150:2.
[2] Lk. 1:49.

JEWISH BELIEF AT THE TIME OF CHRIST

true God. He was not a polytheist; he was a monotheist. So the God that Nicodemus is referring to is not just any god that might exist, but the only true God that does exist. He, then, is already living a life that is pleasing to God, at least in some aspects of it, *before* he believes in Jesus.

Fourth, Nicodemus connected Jesus' mighty deeds to a divine purpose as well as to a divine source. God's divine purpose is brought out in Nicodemus' words *signs* and *teacher*. The miracles that Jesus was performing were not just wonders to be marveled over; they were *signs* pointing to further significant truths. And Nicodemus and those he represented figured that Jesus came *as a teacher* to explain the signs and not simply to amaze His audiences with them.

Ten times in the *Book of Exodus* God performed His miracles so that the Egyptians would know that He alone is the Lord God[1] and that there is none like Him.[2] And if God really is sovereign with no one to prevent Him from accomplishing His purposes, as Job affirms,[3] does this not lead us to suspect that every Egyptian who received the truth to which the ten plagues pointed also became pleasing to God? Interesting question.

...

Jesus didn't come to a nation of "unbelievers" who did not know God or who did not possess an experiential relationship with Him; He came to a nation that already knew God but wasn't living righteously.

...

Nicodemus obtained his worldview from his study of the OT. When God performed miracles, they were done to teach people about Himself. The teacher of Israel was ready to learn

---

[1] E.g., Ex. 7:5, 17; 8:22; 10:2; 14:4, 18.
[2] Ex. 8:10: 9:14.
[3] Cf., Job. 42:2.

from the greater Teacher who had come from God. Whether Nicodemus saw Jesus as the long awaited Teacher of Righteousness[1] that the Qumran Community wrote about is conjecture from a Biblical standpoint. But Jesus was certainly recognized as a teacher from God; that fact is *explicitly* confirmed for us.

If Nicodemus responded in faith to the God of Israel, would you expect him to be *pleasing to God* just as Abraham, Isaac, and Jacob had been? And if his life of faith was *already being justified by God as the patriarchs' lives had been,*[2] what was he learning about and in need of when he was speaking to Jesus?

Jesus knew what was in the heart of every man,[3] right? Consequently, He knew what was in Nicodemus' heart. It should be obvious then that He would not have been offering Nicodemus what He knew Nicodemus already possessed.

If initial *acceptance* by God (if there is such a thing), *justification, regeneration,* and *salvation* are made synonyms (in the sense that they take place at the same instant in time, and refer to different aspects of the same phenomenon), then Nicodemus couldn't have been accepted or justified by God already. Jesus was requiring him to be regenerated[4] (or born again) when He offered him eternal life[5] to save him.[6] But if initial acceptance with God (if there is such a thing), justification, regeneration, and salvation are different matters, which do not necessarily take place at the same point, then it is possible, even

---

[1] Cf., e.g., Isa. 30:20.
[2] This is the point of Hebrews eleven.
[3] John 2:23-25.
[4] John 3:3, 5.
[5] John 3:14-16.
[6] John 3:17. Notice that this salvation is temporal. It concerns life on the earth, not a place with God in heaven.

most likely, that Nicodemus already had *a relationship with God,* but he was still in need of *being regenerated* presently and *saved into the kingdom* whenever it is finally established upon the earth.

I don't expect the reader to understand the distinctions between these terms yet. But the point that must be grasped here is these terms are very different and do not indicate phenomena that occur at the same time. Jesus came to a people who not only believed that the one, true God existed, but that He was a rewarder of those who diligently sought Him. Jesus came to bring these exact persons new resources to handle the new rules of engagement between God and His great adversary as other cultures would be confronted with the claims of Jesus. For it seems rather plain that the spiritual warfare between God and Satan intensified upon the coming of Jesus. And after Jesus' ascension the confrontation with Gentile cultures would prove to be trying. With these new resources, gained from trusting in Jesus, they would be *temporally saved* from the ravages of their personal sins[1] and from the schemes and temptations of the Devil[2] while they would be equipped to engage all the cultures of the world.

By his own words, then, it is rather clear that Nicodemus, whose belief in God had greatly influenced his life, recognized Jesus as someone whom his God had sent to the nation to teach it about His unfolding plans.

If Jesus had not appeared when He did, or if Nicodemus had died before ever meeting Jesus, would we not believe that he would have gone to heaven when he died?

Was he any different from Abraham, Isaac, or Jacob?

---

[1] Matt. 1:21.
[2] Cf., e.g., Eph. 6:10-18.

Did he not believe in the one, true God?

Was he not loving God, as the *Shema* commanded him to do, by teaching others to obey God's Law?

Was he not responding to the miracles that Jesus was performing?

Was not the purpose of Jesus' miracles to lead people to faith in Him as the Messiah[1] that the God of Israel had sent?

Nicodemus was on the right path already. He understood that he was being confronted with new revelation that his God was giving in a person claiming to be the Messiah. And it appeared that Nicodemus was well on his way to receive that new revelation even in the face of lethal peer pressure. *Nicodemus was being illumined, however, not converted.*

Let me illustrate the historical situation that existed in the first century during Jesus' earthly ministry. Let's assume that a person in the first century had to believe in the God of Israel, who was sending a Messiah, for him to be pleasing to God. Furthermore, let's say that a multitude of people had believed in God and in His Messiah who was hopefully coming soon. Now this multitude of people heard of a young teacher named Jesus, and they wanted to go to hear Him, wondering whether He might be the Messiah that they were expecting God to send to them. While they were traveling to the place where He was teaching, they were killed by marauders. According to the old paradigm, where would they have gone after they died? Heaven? Hell?

Now let's assume that some of this same believing multitude managed to escape the marauders and made it to hear Jesus. And He gave His bread of life sermon, designating Himself as

---

[1] Cf., e.g., John 10:37-38.

JEWISH BELIEF AT THE TIME OF CHRIST

the bread out of heaven who was able to give life to all who received Him.[1] While many wanted to make Him king,[2] half of them were not convinced so they rejected His message. After all, His sermon was admittedly not only a hard one to understand but also a difficult one to receive.[3] They then began their return trip home when the marauders come back to finish their job. They all died. Now where would they go?

Would those who believed that Jesus was the Messiah finally be guaranteed heaven?

Would those who rejected Jesus, even though they had believed that their God was sending a Messiah to be their Savior, now be assigned to hell?

...

Does the Bible really teach the need for a "right standing" before God?

...

The old paradigm, that is, orthodox Christian teaching, has no answer for this historical dilemma. It must believe its own *assumptions* without Scriptural support.

Can a person with whom God was pleased in the first century lose his relationship with God by rejecting Jesus even though his faith in God remained strong?

Can the person that God *unconditionally* reckons to be His sons ever produce a *condition* that revokes His reckoning?

...

*Is a **right standing** gained at a point, and then is it good for eternity?*

...

---

[1] John 6:32-33, 47.
[2] John 6:14-15.
[3] John 6:35-36, 60-66.

Does our belief system require that all, who had believed in the God of Israel and in the Messiah that He had promised to send, had to receive Jesus by some logical necessity when He presented Himself?

Nicodemus believed what most agree was necessary to believe to be acceptable to God. And his life certainly exemplified his relationship with God. He was what Jesus wished all the other religious leaders would be. He exemplified Noah before the flood and Abraham after it. In his day he lacked nothing for spiritual acceptability with God.

But with Jesus a new day was dawning. So now he must receive what Jesus was offering or become *less useful* to the God that he believed in and loved.

Nicodemus portrays the elder son in Jesus' *Parable of the Prodigal Son* except he is what Jesus hoped all elder sons would be! To see some inadequacy in Nicodemus' faith before he met Jesus on that fateful evening is to mistake the ever-appearing mirage, created by a preconceived theology, for Biblical reality.

The Samaritan woman at the well

Most Christians have been exposed to the history of the Jewish people and to their antipathy toward the Samaritans. It isn't just that the Samaritans represent those tribes that had separated from the southern tribes during the reign of Solomon's son, Rehoboam, though that is part of it.[1]

It isn't just that they were conquered by the Assyrians and had intermarried with Gentiles that had been transplanted into Samaria (and into the other regions that had been a part of the entire Northern Kingdom), though that is part of it too.[2]

---

[1] 1Kgs. 12–2Kgs. 16 give the relevant history spoken of here.

This antipathy was mainly due to the fact that during the rebuilding of the temple and later of the walls of Jerusalem after the southern tribes had returned from exile, the Samaritans were a constant hindrance to their rebuilding projects.[1] They even went to the extreme of having the King of Medo-Persia give a decree that forced the Jews to stop rebuilding the temple for a time.[2] By the time of Christ nearly five hundred years had elapsed since their return from exile, but the antipathy had only grown more intense between the Jews and the interracial peoples living in Samaria.

When Jesus met the Samaritan woman at the well, He offered her eternal life. Unfortunately, many misunderstand what eternal life is and to what it was connected in the first century. In the same way, this woman did not understand everything He was saying, but she definitely wanted whatever it was that would keep a person from ever thirsting again. To offer eternal life to a Samaritan should enlighten every so-called evangelist today. This was as exceptional offer as it was prototypical!

As their dialogue continued, she came to realize that Jesus must be a prophet. The topic of the proper place to worship God segued into a discussion about the proper person to worship God. Her inquiry about whether worship could take place on Mount Gerizim (in the region of Samaria) or on Mount Moriah (on which Jerusalem had been built) naturally led Jesus to describe the kind of worshipper a person must be since worship is a matter of the heart and not a matter of place.

---

[2] 2Kgs. 16—17 give the history spoken of here.
[1] The books of *Ezra, Nehemiah,* and *Esther* contain the relevant history.
[2] Ezra 3:8—4:24.

Had she confused the offering of sacrifices with worship? That is a possibility. Jerusalem, indeed, was the only place for sacrifices to be offered according to the Jewish Scriptures,[1] but such offerings were only one form of worship. Worship ought to be the natural effervescence of praise from the human heart upon the contemplation of God. The worshipper that God seeks must be a person capable of worshipping in spirit and in truth.[2] Since worship ought to be true all through the day, the place could not be the primary concern.

Jesus told the woman at the well that she worshipped what she didn't (fully) understand. But it is clear that she had some of the facts about God and His promised Messiah correct. The Jews, on the other hand, worshipped what they did understand, namely, that salvation would come out of the Jewish people. What He meant for her to understand is that the deliverance from all of their oppressors would come from the Messiah that God would send all men from the Jewish people. Worship should not only be pure, it must also be according to the truth of God's revelation.[3] The Samaritans had compromised that truth over time.

Continuing the topic about salvation, the Samaritan woman said,

> "*I know the Messiah is coming,* He who is called Christ; when that One comes, He will declare all things to us." (John 4:25, emphasis mine)

Her statement reveals both her knowledge and her humility. She knows that the Jewish Messiah is coming, the one who is called the Christ. How does she know this? The Jews at this time were

---

[1] Cf., e.g., Deut. 14:23, 24, 25; 16:2, 6, 7, 11, 15, 16.
[2] John 4:23-24.
[3] Jesus taught this when He taught on prayer in Matt. 6:9-10.

not known for their evangelistic endeavors; that was especially true relative to the Samaritans. Jesus doesn't tell us who did the sowing before He and His disciples got to Samaria, but He does tell us that someone did. As a result, He and His disciples were entering into someone else's harvest.[1]

Regardless of how she came to her opinion -- her persuasion,[2] yes, her faith[3] -- she knew that the Messiah was coming. It is fairly obvious to the objective person that in a context like this one, *knowing* something that is going to happen is synonymous with *believing* that the thing will happen. Consequently, this lady not only believed in the God of Israel, she also believed in the Messiah that Israel's God was going to send. What is lacking in her faith then? I submit to you that nothing is lacking. She most definitely had a relationship with God *before* trusting in Jesus.

When the woman goes back into town to tell all the townsfolk about Jesus, she asks,

> "This one (who told me all the things that I have done) is not the Christ, is He?" (John 4:29)

While grammatically this question may expect "no" as an answer, yet contextually the woman was working the crowd for a "yes" answer. This is the reason that the men flooded out of the city to meet the person described by the woman. If she was really wanting the men to whom she was witnessing to agree that the man in question couldn't be the Messiah, why do the men all follow her out of the city to meet him?

---

[1] John 4:35-38.
[2] Cf., Acts 17:2-3, 11-12; 18:4, 12-13.
[3] Cf., Acts 28:23-24. ***Being persuaded is believing*** while not being persuaded is remaining in unbelief. Such passages as these in Acts help the student to understand that the nature of faith is a mental phenomenon only.

Another reason contextually to suspect that a "yes" answer was being sought by the woman even though the grammar of her initial question expected their denial is that when we read the men's later comments, we are told that *whatever she had said to them caused them to believe that the one she had met by the well was indeed the Messiah*. The overall context *forces* the reader to understand that the witness the woman gave attempted to prove that He must be the promised Messiah.

But her newly formed belief in Jesus creates for us the same dilemma that we faced when we attempted to understand Nicodemus' spiritual condition at the time he went to Jesus at night. If the woman had already believed in the Messiah, she had to believe in the God who had promised to send Him. After all, the Messiah of Israel was God's anointed. By believing that the God of Israel was sending a Messiah, she would have been *pleasing* to God in that belief just as Abraham had been pleasing to God in believing in God's promise of a multitudinous progeny.

What, then, was Jesus offering her that she did not already have? How was her spiritual state or condition or relationship to God different **before** she believed in Jesus than it was **after** she believed?

The Samaritan woman's dilemma seems to *force* a truth upon us: *a knowledge of God and a relationship with Him are not the same thing as having the eternal life that Jesus offered.* A person can have a relationship with God and live a life that is pleasing to Him and yet not have received the eternal life that comes to a person who believes in Jesus. Having a *relationship* with God, even if one's usefulness to Him is extremely limited because of sin in his life, is not dependent upon having eternal life. The *life* Jesus was offering comes only through faith in Him.

Although the Samaritan woman believed that a Messiah was coming, she needed to believe throughout the rest of her life that Jesus was that Messiah in order to have the salvation about which Jesus spoke. Continuing trust in Jesus to save her from her personal sins and from the trials and temptations of life was needed to obtain the salvation that would deliver her into the future Messianic Kingdom. But if she had rejected Jesus as the Messiah that she knew was coming, that rejection would not have nullified her previous faith in God or made it somehow ineffective. But she would not be able to enter the kingdom in her mortal body if it had been established in her lifetime.

If those comments are confusing, they are so because a false assumption has been made about the meaning of salvation. We must realize that salvation does not refer to going to heaven or to being forgiven of one's sins. It refers to the blessings of partaking in the kingdom that Jesus offered. A righteous life was the condition for entering that kingdom (having *that* salvation).

Jesus was offering something more than what all the believers in God possessed before His ministry began. He was offering her, among other things, eternal life. This life would enable her, if she availed herself of it, to live a spiritually victorious life. She would finally be able to make spiritual, godly decisions, and have the virtue and power to carry them out in the area of her personal relationships with men. Her greatest heartaches could be healed, and her greatest embarrassments could be left behind. The life Jesus was offering her could change her lifestyle completely if she learned how to appropriate – how to live by - that new life! Whenever she drank the water that He was offering her, she would never thirst for anything else. His water gave life!

If she believed in Jesus, accepting thereby the eternal life that He was offering, her relationship with God would not be any more than it already was. If she rejected Jesus, her relationship with God would not be nullified or, somehow, proven to have been an illusion. What Jesus was offering was the means of enjoying her relationship with God at a level she had not experienced before.

The nobleman and his household

The nobleman spoken of in John four was a royal official who lived in Cana where Jesus' first *sign* had been performed. Whether he had been at the wedding or had heard about Jesus' miracle after the fact, we don't know. It appears at first blush that when he learned that Jesus was back in Galilee from His trip to Judea, he made his way to Him to ask Him to heal his son. But it may not be as simple as that. There may have been a little manipulation through negotiation involved as well.

When the nobleman finally succeeds in getting before Him, Jesus rebuked him for some reason. He told the whole crowd that had gathered around Him something that must be related to the father's initial request of Jesus. He said,

> "Unless you [pl. for "you all" or "you people"] see ***signs*** and ***wonders***, you simply ***will not believe***." (John 4:48, emphases and bracket mine)

What is the easiest and simplest way to connect the father's request for healing of his son and Jesus' rebuke? Since the *Book of John* was written to record the *signs* that Jesus performed to lead people to faith in Him as the Messiah, and since the father and his whole household believed in Jesus after the healing of his son, and finally, since this miracle was called Jesus' second *sign*, it is consistent to believe that the father came to Jesus with a bargain in mind. He came to negotiate a bit. He would believe in Jesus as the Messiah **IF** Jesus would heal his son.

Jesus responded to the father's approach with a gentle rebuke. It was gentle because Jesus performed His miracles for the purpose of leading people to faith in Him. This fact Jesus declared quite plainly throughout His ministry. And this is exactly what takes place here in this episode. Nevertheless, Jesus would teach His apostles later that faith in Him apart from seeing miracles is more blessed.[1] So while God may allow a person to negotiate with Him at times, He wants him to understand that He is training him to maintain faith in Him at all times whether or not he sees miracles from His hand.

This father, then, believed that Jesus could be doing miracles in order to prove that He was the Messiah as He clearly claimed to be doing. This meant that the father also believed in the God of Israel because it was only Israel's God who had promised to send a Messiah to Israel in the first place. So the father told Jesus that if He would heal his son, he would believe that *his* God had sent Him to be the promised Messiah.

...

The nobleman does not transition
from an eternally condemned person
to an eternally saved person
by his faith in Jesus.

...

Possessing the same faith in the one, true God as Abraham

---
[1] John 20:26-29. Cf., also John 10:40-41; 2Pet. 1:16-21.

his forefather had, this loving father had already built a relationship with God *before* he came to Jesus. He was now considering whether to accept the new revelation that was being given by his God through the Messiah that He had sent.[1] But he wanted more proof; he wanted God's intervention in his son's life. If he could get that, he would believe that Jesus was the Christ (or Messiah), the Son of God.

As the student of Scripture reads to the end of this episode, he is *forced* to see two different beliefs expressed by the father. One related to the healing of his son; the other related to accepting Jesus as the Christ, the Son of God. When John the apostle tells us that this healing was the second *sign* that Jesus performed (that is, the second one that he recorded for his readers), and when we relate the significance of the *signs* to John's own purpose statement in John 20:31, we are *forced* to believe that Jesus' condescension to the needs of this father led him to faith in His person. That is the reason the apostle John recorded this encounter, and we must accept it in the way John intended it: *faith in the promised miracle fulfilled led to faith in the promised Messiah.*

This father was not worried about becoming certain that he would go to heaven when he died. No Jew would have been. His concern was about living a life that pleased his God now. If he did, all the questions about life after death, if there were any, would take care of themselves.

...

Obtaining eternal life through faith in Jesus is unrelated to obtaining heaven as one's eternal destiny.

...

---

[1] Cf., Heb. 1:1-3.

When he believed that Jesus was the Messiah, he obtained eternal life. This life, confusingly termed *eternal* life, is not at all about eternity; it is about time; it is about the quality of life one can live while he continues to pursue fellowship with God daily.

The father already believed in the God of Israel like his forefather Abraham had done. To the extent that he was faithful in his walk with God, he enjoyed the blessings of God and will be rewarded with a future salvation, which involves a place of service in the Messiah's kingdom when He returns to set it up.

But the point not to be missed is that Jesus' offer of eternal life was different from and in addition to what he already possessed. He is given eternal life for the purpose of living a righteous life with the hope of entering the salvation that comes from the Jews through their Messiah.

...

Jesus did not come to replace faith in the Father with faith in the Son.

...

If he had never come to Jesus in the first place, or if he had refused to believe in Jesus after his son was healed, his relationship with God would not have been affected at all. *Jesus never presented Himself as an object of faith that competed with or superseded a person's faith in the God of Israel, Jesus' heavenly Father.* In fact, He was very careful to explain that when a person believed in Him, there was a continuity rather than a discontinuity to what was already believed. Jesus said it this way:

"... he who believes in Me does not believe in Me ..." (John 12:44a)

Now if that statement doesn't grab your attention, then you may be in a spiritual stupor or just plain dull of hearing. This is Jesus' way of saying that He didn't come to start something new. *He came to fulfill the OT faith, not replace it!* So, the rest of that verse says this:

> "… he who believes in Me does not believe in Me, but in Him [the Father!] who sent Me." (John 12:44, bracket mine)

Jesus is saying that He didn't come to create a "new faith" or a new religion. He came to give further reasons why faith in God the Father and in His everlasting covenants and promises ought to be maintained. Some of the truths that spring from this reality are:

> Believing in Jesus is not better than believing in the Father.
> Believing in Jesus is not an additional requirement for being acceptable to the Father.
> Believing in Jesus doesn't secure anything more in the afterlife than believing in the Father did.
> Believing in Jesus is a continuation of faith in the Father.

The old windowpane tended to distort or obscure these truths.

Jesus came to affirm the validity of faith in the Father; He came to bolster that faith, not replace it with a faith in Himself. To place Jesus above the Father by requiring a person to have faith in Jesus as a condition for having a relationship with the Father is to misunderstand why Jesus came in the first place.

The healed lame man[1]

The lame man had been in his illness for 38 years. That does not mean that he had been at the pool of Bethesda for that entire time. But his presence there after 38 years of enduring his sickness, does tell us several things. First, it tells us that he

---
[1] John 5:1-17.

believed the legend that God would send down an angel to stir up the waters in the pool for the purpose of healing the first one that entered the pool. This leads us to think that he believed that the God of Israel was a good and merciful God who remained in the midst of His people,[1] giving them continual evidences of His presence and His goodness. That is both reasonable and Scriptural as I demonstrated earlier.

Second, it tells us that he apparently believed that some of the people around that pool were actually healed during his time there. Why else would he want to be at the pool and lie around it with all the other afflicted, sick persons? If no one ever got healed, he and others would have figured that out and would have come to believe that the legend was nothing more than a fairy tale, a myth, and a cruel one at that. But there he was along with a multitude of sick, blind, lame, and withered, waiting for the waters to be stirred.

I realize that the whole crowd around that pool could have been deceived. I understand that they may have been self-deluded in their obsession to be healed just like many are today who participate in various healing ministries. But there is one major difference between the people around the pool of Bethesda and the defrauding ministries found today: there was no middleman who gained anything from the successes that occurred at the pool of Bethesda. There was no preacher or evangelist or miracle worker who received an honorarium or fame or credibility from the healing that was supposed to have happened. There were only the sick people and their God; and only God got the glory. It did not take great faith to be healed; it

---

[1] Cf., supra pp. 107-08, 118-120.

took a great God who cares for His people. Such is the God of Israel.

...

Whatever happened around that pool reflected upon the character of God, the God in whom they all, apparently, already believed in.

...

Not only did they believe in God, they were daily trusting Him to send another angel to stir up the water. And I understand about the underground spring that *may have had* an affect upon the pool. But that might be nothing more than the secondary means God chose to stir up the water. The fact that multitudes continued to come and to wait for the stirring of the water implies what the man specifically believed: *some people at different times actually got well!*

While the lame man had limited God to just this one means of healing him, he obviously wanted to be healed. After he received his healing, where do we find him? In the temple offering the Law's required sacrifice for his purification.

What does this tell us about the man? He believed in the God of Israel who gave his nation the Law. Having just been healed by that God, he went to give thanks by offering the sacrifice his God required. Since he believed in the God of Israel, he was following in the footsteps of Abraham his forefather and in the footsteps of all the saints listed in the eleventh chapter of the Book of Hebrews. *As he lived by faith, he pleased the God of his faith*. As he walked by faith, God approved of every step he took.

Jesus presented Himself to him as the long-awaited Messiah whom, apparently, he refused to accept. Rather than believe in

Jesus, he betrayed Jesus into the hands of some of the religious leaders who had already rejected Him.

...

In this healed man, we have an example of a "believer" in the God of Israel not accepting the Messiah!

...

By rejecting Jesus, he committed *the unpardonable sin*, the consequences of which have nothing to do with his eternal destiny, but everything to do with obtaining the blessings and promises that Jesus was offering. We will discuss the unpardonable sin in some detail later on.

Here then is a man who believed in the God of Israel and, if we are consistent with the message of the Scriptures, was pleasing to God every time he responded to the revelation that God gave him. Just as many of the religious leaders were doing, the healed lame man believed in the God of Israel, trusted in Him daily, but rejected Jesus without endangering or destroying the relationship that he already enjoyed with God. Once again, *Jesus came to enhance the OT faith in the God of Israel, not to replace it with a faith in Himself.*

...

One can know God, be attempting to obey Him, and yet reject Jesus as the Messiah.

...

As in the cases of Nicodemus, the Samaritan woman, and the nobleman, would we not agree that if the lame man had died before he met Jesus, he would have been welcomed or accepted by God since he believed in God and was obeying Him according to the light and ability that he had? I would.

Jesus came to give a life that enables each person, who receives it, to be a super-conqueror in spiritual issues.[1]

He came to enable all prodigals to overcome the sins that have ensnared them.[2] In this most important sense, He came to be man's *Savior*. He had not come to save anyone from hell or to promise him heaven. But He had come to equip every man with a life that could overcome every obstacle to personal righteousness.

An overview of the rest of Jesus' addressees

Every person and every group of people, including all the religious leaders of Jesus' day, that Jesus encountered in the *Gospel of John* believed in the one, true God, and were, to various degrees, attempting to obey His Law in order to please Him.

The multitude of 5,000 trusted in God.
The religious leaders trusted in God.
The blind man and his parents trusted in God.
Even Judas trusted in God.

All of them believed in God, but none did so perfectly. All of them believed in God, but were still self-centered at times. All of them believed in God and attempted to obey Him just like all of the patriarchs in the OT. They were not better off if they accepted Jesus, nor were they worse off if they rejected Him *relative to obtaining in the after-life a heavenly place with God*. We know this is true because Jesus only sought to *enhance people's faith in the Father* exactly as the OT had taught the Jewish people to do before Jesus came. Setting aside the Mosaic Law because it

---

[1] Rom. 8:37.
[2] Matt. 1:21; 1John 3:5-6.

had become fulfilled relative to the coming of Messiah is not the same thing as setting aside the OT faith in God. The Jewish faith was never meant to be forsaken.

Chapter 10

The Unpardonable Sin

One of the natural questions arising from the line of thinking in this book is "What would have been true of any first century person who was filling the conditions of Heb. 11:6 but, who, nevertheless, rejected Jesus?"

Since he already believed in God and was allowing that belief to impact his life to some degree, what would he have lost if he had refused to believe in Jesus?

Would his unbelief have cost him heaven?

Would he have been consigned to an eternity in hell?

What would have been the consequences upon that first century person if he not only walked with the God of Israel, but had believed in a coming Messiah?

What would the pronouncements have been upon his faith *before* he encountered Jesus?

Would he have lost heaven because he refused to believe in Jesus even though he had continued to believe in the God of Israel and in His coming Messiah?

Years ago these questions occurred to me, and I let them slip by without thinking very deeply about them. Neither the questions nor the answers that I initially gave to them fit very well into my overall system of thinking at the time. As a result, I dismissed them, assuming the unlikely, if not impossible, position that every believer in God, who was attempting to obey Him the best he could, would have believed in the Messiah when He finally appeared. Because I believed in the traditional dichotomies of *believer/unbeliever* and *heaven/hell* and *lost/saved* that are usually taught, I had no place for those who didn't fit into those neat little categories. As a result, these questions kept goading me to make some mid-course corrections. When God's goading began to be felt at every turn, I finally responded.

Can a person please God today in the same way, for example, that Abraham did in his day?

Can a person find approval with God today in the same way that Joseph did?

These questions help us to answer the previous questions.

If believing in God, apart from almost any cogent information about God's coming Messiah, was adequate in the OT, is there any reason that it would not be sufficient today?

As one reads the OT, it seems quite plain that until the days of the prophets very little, if anything, was known about the coming Messiah. That information simply had not been revealed yet. So, could someone today believe in the one, true God without believing in the Messiah that He has sent, and still be acceptable or welcomed to God?

The knee jerk reaction, I know, is a response similar to this one: "Well, Jesus changes everything! You must believe in Him to have a relationship and walk with God today." But did Jesus really come to *change* everything? Or did He, as I argued in the last chapter, come to *fulfill* what His heavenly Father had promised to do for those *who already believed in Him* (i.e., already believed in the Father)? The will of God revealed in the OT, whether it came directly from the Father or through Jesus' preincarnate theophanies or even through other agencies, angelic or human, circumscribed the plan the Father wanted accomplished by Jesus in His earthly ministry. That should be our focus.

Because we have isolated Jesus from His true role of representing,[1] explaining,[2] and fulfilling[3] the Father's[4] will, we tend to substitute other roles, goals, and purposes for Him in place of the true ones.

...

Jesus came to fulfill the will of God, not to change it in any way.

...

That is the reason we have such things as "Replacement Theology," a doctrine that believes that the Church replaces Israel as God's people, leaving no place or need for the nation of Israel in God's continuing plan for mankind. It is also the reason we have amillennialism and postmillennialism, the doctrines that say that there will not be any physical kingdom established upon this earth. The kingdom promised to King David's descendants has been revoked because of Israel's sins.

...

*Some current doctrines would be impossible to hold
if Jesus was connected to the OT as its literal fulfiller.*

...

As I finally began to give the previous questions more thought, being forced to do so by God's orchestration of *many buffeting goads* in my life, I eventually realized, by the grace of God and the illumination of His Spirit, how unnatural and unrealistic it is to believe that every believer in the God of Israel

---

[1] Heb. 1:3; John 14:7-9.
[2] John 1:18.
[3] John 17:4; Heb. 10:7.
[4] Matt. 6:10.

in the first century would have received Jesus as the promised Messiah. The more open I became and the more willing I became to question the presuppositions upon which some of my beliefs rested, the more some classic verses began to lead me in a different direction. These verses confirmed the truthfulness of the view that *God's people had indeed rejected God's Messiah in the first century*. This truth, once accepted, allowed verses to say to me what they were always intended to say, but what I was unwilling to have them say until I began to respond to the clear declarations of Scripture.

My theological conditioning closed me off from every principle, concept, or developed doctrine that contradicted my own theological system. That would not be a bad thing if my system were infallible. But to my chagrin, it wasn't. Nor has it become so today. I'm still learning as I become more sensitive to God's illumining Spirit. As a result, I am slowly overcoming my theological training that had blinded me to every possibility that veered from the theology that I had been taught.

For example, in attempting to answer the question about the possibility that any of God's people could have actually rejected Jesus in the first century, I was blind to what the apostle John was trying to communicate when he penned John 1:11-12. It says,

> "***He came to*** His own [things] and ***those who were His own [people] did not receive Him***. But as many as did received Him, to them He gave the right to *be* children of God, even to those who believe in His name." (author's translation, emphases and brackets)

Jesus came to *His own people*; He came to those who already believed in His Father and to various degrees were walking with

Him. *But most of His own people did not receive Him as the Messiah sent from God.*

…

*Many of God's chosen people in the first century
committed the unpardonable sin.*

…

Those that did receive Him were given the privilege of *being* children *of God*. This privilege was (and still is) a dynamic issue, rather than a static one. As they walked by faith, they manifested their sonship. When they didn't walk by faith, they didn't manifest their privileged relationship to the Father. In both cases, they were still sons with a relationship with the Father. One living a vital life; the other having a lifeless existence at times.

…

*Although the Jews in the first century already belonged to God
and could, therefore, be called His people,
they received the new birth only when they believed in Jesus.*

…

Matthew tried to explain these same issues to me in the opening chapter of the Gospel that he wrote, but I was simply not putting the pieces together properly. When Matthew recorded the angel's message to Joseph concerning Mary's baby, he explained that the angel's revelation had a particular focus. He said,

> "Joseph, son of David, do not be afraid to take Mary your wife; for that which has been conceived in her is of the Holy Spirit. And she will bear a Son; and you shall call His name ***Jesus***, for it is He ***who will save His people from their sins***." (Matt. 1:20-21, emphases mine)

Joseph was told to give their baby the name Jesus, a name that means *Savior*, in light of the work that He would attempt to accomplish. Jesus was coming to *save* His people! Did you catch that? Jesus came to save *those who already had a relationship to God*. He came to save the people that we are typically call *believers*. He came to save *His people*, the Jew who believed in God and who was trying to obey Him as the Shema instructed him to do.

The second truth that Matthew set before his readers is the object from which the people were to be saved. Jesus came to save His people *from their sins*. That is, He came to save the people of Israel from their sinful habits and passions. Consequently, the very first mention of salvation in the NT dealt with *the personal life of believers* while they lived that life on this earth. It had no connection at all to heaven or hell or to any aspect of the afterlife. This salvation was a promise of deliverance from the sins that were enslaving the people of God. And if God's people, that is, those individuals who entertained a continuous, but inconsistent, relationship with God, needed saving, it should be obvious that this need must have a universal application.

Israel in the first century, just like believers today, needed to be saved from their sinful lifestyles. This does not mean that they were grossly immoral although that too is a possibility. Rather, it means that *they had learned to live moral lives, for the most part, apart from being the servants of God that they ought to have been*. They were worldly and legalistic at the same time. They were conformed to the world and yet committed to the external demands of their faith simultaneously.

Consequently, both John the baptizer and Jesus came on the scene preaching repentance. This was exactly what they needed to do! They needed to repent, but not for the purpose of being saved from hell. They needed to repent so that they could be saved from their personal sins by the *life* Jesus would give them. That *life* could overcome their sins and give them an experience of a wonderful, blessed life in the process.

The goads God was using on me led me to revisit a lot of issues, finally bringing me back to the matter of the unpardonable sin. This sin, I discovered, has nothing to do with going to heaven or missing hell. This sin pertains to the issue of the kingdom program Jesus was preaching. To deny that Jesus was the promised Messiah and, therefore, had the authority to offer and to set up the long-awaited kingdom promised to David's seed was to commit the unpardonable sin[1] in the first century. But the important point to see here is this: the unpardonable sin is committed only by those whom we would call *believers*.

As Jesus ministered, He offered the kingdom and taught about the requirements for its establishment. As He did this, the Holy Spirit convicted the hearts of all who heard Him preach the OT passages, concepts, and principles related to that kingdom. *To reject the Spirit's conviction on this message was to commit the unpardonable sin.* This sin is kingdom related.

This sin, Jesus plainly said, is not forgiven in the present age. The present age is a reference to the time during which Jesus was on earth ministering personally. The next age, when Biblical chronology is being considered, is the millennial kingdom during which Jesus will be ruling physically on the earth as a king over all peoples and things. The unpardonable sin of rejecting Jesus as Messiah-King in the first century resulted in

---

[1] Matt. 12:28 is the key to understanding the unpardonable sin (Matt. 12:31-32).

Israel's destruction by Rome. The Messiah, who would have saved Israel from the hand of all who were hating them at the time, delayed the establishment of the kingdom and allowed the destruction of Israel's nation because of Israel's rejection of Him. From the consequences of this sin, there would be no reprieve.

While the Jewish rejecters were kept from *seeing* the kingdom established and from *entering* the kingdom in their mortal bodies during the first century,[1] they could still have a part in the kingdom if they qualified for it by righteously living at their resurrection when they obtained their new, glorified bodies. The unpardonable sin was only warning the Jews of a postponement of the kingdom due to their sin and forbidding their immediate entrance into it with their mortal bodies. But if they would otherwise live a righteous life, they would serve Him in His kingdom at the restoration of all things.

In short then, the unpardonable sin in the first century, called *the present age* by Jesus, is a rejection of Jesus as God's Messiah during His personal ministry. The penalty for that rejection was a delay in establishing the kingdom and the inability of the rejecters to enter the kingdom in their mortal bodies. The unpardonable sin in the age to come (i.e., during the millennial reign of Messiah) is also a rejection of Jesus as God's Messiah. The penalty for that rejection will again be physical death and the removal of the rejecter from the kingdom that he had been a part of.

In the first century, those who rejected Jesus brought upon themselves their own destruction by the hands of their enemies, the Romans. During the millennial reign of Jesus, those who reject Him will bring upon themselves their own physical death

---

[1] Cf., Jesus' admonition to Nicodemus in John 3:3, 5.

by Jesus Himself and a commensurate chastisement after death. In both cases, the immediate consequence will be the same: physical death.

Chapter 11

Distinguishing Acceptance, Justification, and Salvation

Sometimes we must push against the walls of our paradigms in order to test them. Sometimes our push reveals to us that it is time to abandon our paradigms and adopt new ones. It is not the purpose of this book to be technical, but general, so that every Christian can understand what the Bible is about and be better equipped to study it effectively on his own. The definitions that follow, then, are meant to be general as well … general but Biblically demanded!

Acceptance by God

In my first several drafts of this book, I argued for and attempted to explain how a person is *initially accepted* by God. By the process of elimination, I presumably identified the consequences of initial faith. I tried my best to defend what I had been taught. My arguments, I now realize, were *inferential* and *conjectural* at best. By that process of elimination, my research led me to believe that whatever was included in justification, sanctification, salvation, and glorification couldn't be included in a person's *initial acceptance* by God. So logically, all that was not included in those doctrines had to fit into the doctrine of initial acceptance with God. There has to be an *initial faith experience* for everyone, right? That was what I had been taught and I didn't see any reason to reject that idea. But I was having trouble discerning exactly what that was that fit there.

Then it was suggested to me finally that maybe the reason that I was having so much trouble identifying examples of *initial faith* and describing what happens at that time is that I'm trying to defend something that can't be found in the Scriptures. Of course, I was initially stunned at the suggestion. But it didn't take me long to admit that my friend's suggestion was exactly what was happening. At first, I simply couldn't believe it!

I had already drawn conclusions consistent with my friend's suggestion from my research into the other doctrines listed above. For example, I had already stated in my manuscript that I couldn't find a single reference of anyone exercising initial faith in all of the OT. Thirty-nine books without one reference to it! So I asked, "Why do you suppose there is no example of initial faith?" I finally gave this true but safe answer: *initial faith must not be that important of a concept if it is never mentioned.* As Sherlock Holmes would have said, "Elementary, my dear Watson! Elementary." My friend fearlessly looked deeper.

The better analysis of that fact of omission is that *there really isn't a point of initial faith for anyone.* If there are no examples of initial faith in the OT, then it is absurd to formulate a doctrine describing what is involved in it or what results from it. No one can know these things since there is no divine revelation on the matter![1]

I have concluded that the theological doctrine of initial faith should be abandoned due to a lack of divine communication about it. God's focus in the revelation that He has given to us is upon *continuing* faith, not *initial* faith. If a person does not

---

[1] Cf., Deut. 29:29; Isa. 55:8-9.

pursue the fulfillment of the purpose for which he was created and placed upon the earth, namely, *to have fellowship with his Creator and to represent Him as he lives by faith*, then God has promised to discipline him for wasting the opportunities he had to do so. Since the Bible never addresses, much less focuses upon, initial faith as is done in men's systematic theologies, is our theological thinking in line with the Scriptures or just a reflection of man's best thinking?

Justification by God

The term justification is typically used to refer to a person's initial faith in God in the OT or to his initial faith in Jesus in the NT. But since there is not one OT instance describing initial faith, this teaching has no Scriptural basis. And if the people that Jesus was addressing throughout His ministry were God's people already, then the faith they exercised in Him could not have been their initial faith either.

…

All theologies that relate justification to initial faith are based on assumptions rather than upon the facts of Scripture.

…

For at least five hundred years it has been assumed that the term justification designates God's declaration over a person's initial response of faith. And in that declaration He *supposedly* pronounces upon the believer a righteous standing or status before God that lasts forever. **It has been assumed** that the Bible is about man doing what is necessary to become eternally acceptable to God. **It has been assumed** that man, *supposedly* having no righteousness of his own, needed a perfect righteousness to be accepted by God. **It has been assumed** that this righteousness comes to man freely through his faith in Jesus in such a way that he can be described as being "clothed in the righteousness of Christ." And when he is clothed with that righteousness, he becomes fully accepted by God forever. Since God is always pleased with His Son, when a person is clothed with His righteousness, He will always be pleased with him.

What this book is suggesting is that *justification has nothing at all to do with a person's presumed initial acceptance with God, and that the Bible does not teach that man even needs such righteousness to be accepted by God.* Even when we encounter examples that might be initial faith in the *Book of Acts*, it is always for *salvation* that they believe, rather than for initial acceptance or for justification. And salvation, as I will explain in a moment, is temporal; it has nothing to do with securing a person's eternal destiny.

Christian pundits endlessly debate the place of works in going to heaven. This focus is the result of looking through the wrong windows into the Scriptures. Each side of the debate has its own window, stained and etched by the church traditions they have found acceptable, as they reteach the conclusions of renowned scholars. Eventually, everyone becomes so far removed from the Scriptures, as they stand behind their stained glass windows, now muddied by hundreds of years of religious debates, that they feel safer quoting past scholars than referring to the Scriptures themselves. They have become content in studying, believing, and quoting the conclusions of their denominational heroes of the faith than relying upon their own studies of God's Word.

The easily proven facts that 1.) justification can't be the result of a person's initial faith and that 2.) justification is not a once-for-all phenomenon demonstrate that the theological paradigm that we have depended upon to guide our Bible study for five hundred years is inadequate. The Biblical doctrine of justification is not what we have been taught it is. And, should God's grace grant it, the next revival will be dependent upon our straightening out this theological confusion.

...

Justification involves works because it is God's evaluation of the works that a person has just done.

...

When God evaluates each work a person commits, He either *commends* it by declaring that it is a righteous response, or He *condemns* it by declaring that it is an unrighteous response. When He commends it, that commendation is properly called justification. If a work is done in faith, it will be reckoned by God as righteous. But only those works that spring from faith will be judged so.[1] Everything else is sinful[2] regardless of how much it may have conformed to the accepted standard of behavior outlined by the Church's traditions or historical, Christian orthodoxy.

Salvation by Jesus

Salvation is a broad term, Biblically speaking. Essentially it refers to a deliverance or to a rescue of some kind. The same Greek terms translated *save* or *salvation* may refer to a variety of *spiritual* deliverances as well as to *non-spiritual* deliverances like healing or being saved from drowning. To assume that the term means the same thing in every context in which it is used is to assure complete confusion in Bible study. *Context is king*.

---

[1] Js. 2:21-24.
[2] Cf., Rom. 14:23. Everything that a person does not in faith is sin.

Whatever the context is dealing with will lead the student of Scripture to the proper meaning of the term in each instance.

The salvation described in the NT is a multi-faceted blessing. There are at least five aspects to it (depending upon how the interpreter breaks it all down). When a person is saved, he is saved from personal sins;[1] or he may be saved from *the present evil age*.[2] He is given *the Holy Spirit*[3] who will oppose indwelling sin[4] and make him *a member* of the invisible, universal Body of Christ. (In connection with the Holy Spirit, but distinct from Him, the person is given access to *a new life in Christ Jesus called eternal life*.[5]) When a person is saved, that salvation may be a reference to a deliverance from *the wrath of God* that is coming upon the earth during the period called the Tribulation.[6] And finally, he is given *the opportunity, if he meets the condition of having lived a righteous life, to eventually be delivered into or saved for the coming earthly kingdom of the Messiah*.[7] The context will delineate which of these aspects of salvation a given author is discussing.

It should be noted that no aspect of salvation listed above deals with the prospect of going to heaven or of escaping hell. Salvation refers to what God had done, is doing, and promises to do for the one who trusts in God as he walks with Him daily. Salvation is about this life, not the hereafter.

---

[1] Matt. 1:21. Cf., 1John 3:5-6.
[2] Cf., Acts 2:40; Gal. 1:1-4.
[3] Acts 2:38; John 7:37-39. Cf., also Mk. 16:15-16.
[4] Gal. 5:16-17. Cf., Rom. 8:1-7 although in that immediate context indwelling sin is referred to as the *flesh* among other things in the broader context of Romans 6-8.
[5] Rom. 6:4-5; John 6:47.
[6] Rom. 5:9; 1Thess. 1:10; 5:8-9.
[7] Matt. 6:33; 19:23-25; 24:13-14; etc.

To be saved then is to be delivered from the sin that so easily entangles us[1] and from the sins that are ruining our lives.[2] To remain a prodigal puts one in eminent danger of experiencing God's discipline. It has always been, and remains to be,

"... a terrifying thing to fall into the hands of the living God." (Heb. 10:31)

To overcome these things we need a Savior. In His love for us He provided more than we need in the resources that are offered freely in Jesus. God stands on the front porch watching for His prodigal sons and daughters who might be coming home. Complete forgiveness, a wonderful relationship, and a staggering inheritance awaits the one who returns.

The book of Romans

The study of the *Book of Romans* makes a good case for the distinction between a *supposedly needed* acceptance with God, justification, and salvation. The audience to whom Paul wrote his letter was described as:

Called of Jesus Christ (1:6)
Beloved of God (1:7)
Called saints (1:7)
Recognized for their active faith in God (1:8)
Brethren (1:13)

Hence, Paul was writing, by his own clear designation, to people *who have maintained some degree of relationship with the only true God and with Jesus Christ whom He had sent into the world*. But these same people still needed both the *justification* that Paul

---

[1] Heb. 12:1-2.
[2] 1Pet. 4:1-6; 2Pet. 2:18-22.

THE PRODIGAL PARADIGM

described in his letter as well as the *salvation* that he distinguished from that justification. These three issues can't be equated.

When I went into the ministry over 49 years ago, one of the most amazing speakers, to whom I was exposed, was Josh McDowell. His favorite verse was Rom. 1:16. It states plainly that the gospel that Paul had in mind when he wrote his letter to the Christians in Rome was a message of salvation to everyone who believes [in Jesus[1]]:

> "For I am not ashamed of **the gospel**, for **it** is the power of God **for salvation** to everyone who **believes**, to the Jew first and also to the Greek." (Rom. 1:16, emphases mine)

Josh would quote that verse every time he spoke and then defend the Christian faith from the various attacks it was currently under. His ministry continues to the glory of God and should be searched out by churches and individual ministries that need to be trained in apologetics as well as in a host of other disciplines. I couldn't recommend him more highly than I do.

Back in my early days of ministry, however, it never occurred to me to test some of the *assumptions* that I brought with me into the study of the Bible. For example, it never occurred to me that the referent for *gospel* in Romans 1:16 might be different from that of 1Cor. 15:3-5. It never entered my mind that the term *gospel* might refer to different things in different contexts.

Likewise, I *presumed* that the term *salvation* was basically related to the concepts of justification, redemption, reconciliation, regeneration, and propitiation, with them all occurring at the same moment of initial faith. I *supposed* that they

---

[1] Cf., Rom. 1:1-8; 10:9-13. This is the context and sense to which Paul is referring.

all referred to some aspect of my great spiritual deliverance from hell by Jesus who paid the price for my sins on the cross so that they could be forgiven and I could be eternally accepted by God. It did not occur to me back then to actually trace the terms for justification gospel, and salvation through the Book of Romans to see how they were used. I *assumed* a point of view that today I regret.

As I began my own journey of reevaluating and restudying the things that I had been taught, I became quite interested in some fascinating messages that I was hearing by seminary and Bible college professors on salvation in the Book of Romans. These piqued my interest because they helped me to deal with some of the more troubling passages in Paul's letter. But still the direction that these messages were going didn't seem to answer all the problems that were present. So I continued to think about those issues for many years.

Then as I began to discern more clearly the truths of the message I'm setting before you in this book, the meanings of the various terms for gospel, justification, and salvation in Romans became almost self-evident. For example, when Paul says that he is not ashamed of the gospel, he is referring to the good news that he is sharing throughout his whole letter to the Roman church. It is obvious, and ought to be beyond debate, that his message to the Roman Christians is not limited to the content of 1Cor. 15:3-5. *In fact, Paul's main concern is about a justification that leads to a future salvation*. This thought process is not dealt with at all in 1Cor. 15. It is gratuitous to think that these two "gospels" can simply be transposed without enormously changing Paul's message to the Romans.

So when Paul singled out salvation in Romans, I had to ask

myself, what exactly is Paul referring to by that term? As I investigated the matter more thoroughly, I noticed that Paul dealt with justification in chapters three and four primarily, but he did not treat salvation until chapter nine, only making two passing references[1] to a (different?) salvation before that time. This again demonstrates that these two issues, justification and salvation, do not refer to the same thing.

In Rom. 5:1, 9 Paul made a couple of clear distinctions for us between these two terms. He says,

> "Therefore **having been justified by faith**, let us have peace with God[2] through our Lord Jesus Christ . . . . Much more then, **having been justified** now by His blood, we **shall be saved** through Him from the wrath." (author's translation and emphases)

We ought to notice first that the justification to which Paul referred had already happened to his audience. Twice he declared that they had been justified already in the past. But the salvation of which he wanted to speak was still a future event. It had not yet happened to them.[3] *Justification was a fact; salvation was a hope. Justification was a completed act by God (a pronouncement or declaration by Him that had already taken place); salvation had not yet finished.*[4] Hence, these two issues must be distinct.

---

[1] Rom. 5:9-10; 8:24.

[2] While this is the marginal reading in the NASV, I believe it is the better reading based upon manuscript evidence and the argument of Paul from Romans five through eight, among several other reasons. The renowned Greek scholar A.T. Robertson, in his Word Pictures in the New Testament, vol. 4, *The Epistles of Paul*. Broadman Press, Nashville, Tennessee, 1931, pp. 355-56, agrees.

[3] Even if the future is taken to be a deliberative future denoting an assured experience at any time even in the present, it still requires a distinction to be made between it and the justification that had already occurred in the past.

[4] If it is a future salvation/deliverance from God's future outpouring of His wrath (see 1Thess. 5:9-10; Rev. 6:17), it has not yet begun. If it is a present salvation/deliverance (see Rom. 1:18), it is not yet finished.

The second distinction that Paul makes between justification and salvation is that justification is based upon the blood or death of Christ while salvation is based upon His life. Paul said it this way:

> "For if while we were enemies, *we were reconciled to God through the death of His Son*, much more, having been reconciled, *we shall be saved by His life*." (Rom. 5:10, emphases mine)

While reconciliation and justification are not the same thing, they do relate to the same thing: *maintaining fellowship with God*.[1] Hence, they both have to do with the death of Christ on the believer's behalf. In the same way that justification is contrasted to salvation in verse nine, reconciliation is contrasted to salvation in verse ten. In other words, **Christ Jesus died** to justify those who believe in Him and to reconcile them to God.

But Jesus *now lives* to accomplish not only the salvation spoken of in Rom. 5:9-10 but also the prophecies of a salvation in the distant future that remain unfulfilled. The prophetic salvation that Paul is referring to is the coming conquest of King Jesus over all of Israel's enemies, delivering (*saving!*) that nation from her enemies and moving her into the safety of His reign upon the earth for a millennium. When he began his letter with his thematic statement,

> "I'm not ashamed of the gospel (of Christ) for it **(He) is the power of God for salvation"** (to bring it, to establish it upon the earth) . . . (Rom. 1:16, author's translation from the Majority Text, emphases, and parentheses)

he was referring to this future event, and not to a "spiritual salvation from hell." In the book of Romans, heaven is never the

---

[1] It should be noted that this is not the traditional view of either of these terms.

reward for faith nor is hell the consequence of a lack of it. Rather, justification is about living righteously now so that the Messiah can return to bring salvation to the earth.

...

Only in chapters nine through eleven of Romans does Paul explain the salvation that he has in mind in his letter to the Romans.

...

And later in his letter when he wrote that "the remnant . . . will be *saved*,"[1] he was not speaking of an *elect remnant of unbelievers*. The saving of an elect but as yet unredeemed group of people is nowhere to be found in the Bible.[2] Paul was actually describing *a remnant of believers* who already possessed a relationship with God and who will be physically saved from their enemies in the future. Paul lifted two verses out of a text from *the Book of Isaiah* that dealt with the Northern Kingdom's defeat and exile by the Assyrians. But all will not be lost since God will bring back a remnant of His exiled people to the Promised Land. In the same way that God preserved His people in the Northern Kingdom at the time of Assyria's conquest of them, He will preserve present day Israel at the end of the coming Great Tribulation. A remnant of Jews, driven out of their land and scattered by the Antichrist, will be rescued and brought back to the Promised Land safely. This is part of the good news, *the gospel*, that Paul wanted to preach to the Christians at Rome.

But don't mistake what I'm saying. This future salvation is *a big part* of his argument; actually it is *the main point* that Paul was

---

[1] Rom 9:27.
[2] Christian orthodoxy, formulated primarily in the sixteenth to the eighteenth centuries, is what I am opposing here. In short, the terms salvation, election, and redemption should be revisited and defined in terms of Biblical usage rather than by how they are used in the theological formulations of the past.

making in his letter to the Roman assemblies. The Jews definitely have a future. But participation in that future salvation is based upon living righteously now just as the Jews in Rome had already surmised from the OT.

This concept of salvation is consistent throughout Paul's letter. Consequently, when Paul prayed for Israel's salvation,[1] he was not praying that they come to *true* faith in the one, *true* God so that they could be *truly* saved from hell. Rather, he acknowledged their zeal for the one, true God, but explained that their zeal was nevertheless misguided. And their deliverance from Gentile domination would not come until their righteousness became what God demanded it should be.

Israel did not understand the difference between the morality that one might have from following God's law and the spirituality that one must have before the Messiah can bring their salvation. Their *righteousness* was one of conformity (but, apparently, not also one of faith). *Paul knew the difference between moral conformity to God's will and a spiritual relationship with God who had given a revelation of His will to Israel.* Since justification is God's declaration of righteousness upon a person's response of faith, conformity without faith does not meet God's standard. It is not a response or lifestyle that He can justify.

Later in the letter to Rome, Paul strove to clarify the salvation that he had in mind. He explained that it comes from a belief and a confession. The Jew must believe that his God raised Jesus from the dead. In the day that Israel responds like Paul is describing, Jesus will return to deliver them from the enemies threating their existence.

---

[1] Rom. 10:1.

It ought to be clear that calling on the name of the Lord is not a requirement for the supposedly eternally condemned and unredeemed man to be spiritually once-for-all redeemed. Calling on the name of the Lord is not the means by which the "unbeliever" becomes a "believer" (using these terms in their traditional, but imprecise sense). *Furthermore, the need to confess is a work that must be done for salvation to come to a person in this context.* Both calling on the name of the Lord and confessing Jesus are the requirements or conditions that must be met for God to send Jesus back to deliver Israel from His wrath being poured out upon the earth in the future days of the Great Tribulation. But meeting these conditions will not, unfortunately, guarantee to a person a destiny in heaven and an escape from hell. That subject simply isn't broached in Romans.

While Rom. 10:13 explicitly says, "Whoever will call upon the name of the Lord will be saved," according to the next verse it is *only believers* who are qualified to make this call. Only after a preacher has been sent and preaches, can a person hear the message that is needful. And only after hearing this message and believing it, is he ready to call upon the name of the Lord for his *physical* salvation. Taking verses nine through thirteen out of Paul's argument and making them stand alone with an errant theology of salvation read into them has blinded the church to Paul's original meaning and intention.

But if we just step back a bit and read the whole of chapters nine through eleven over and over again, we will see that Paul is talking about Israel's future salvation from her enemies. In fact, all that Paul says here ought to sound very much like God's commission of Moses to deliver His people out of Egypt. He had heard their cries ~ their calls ~ to Him about their distresses.[1]

They were calling upon His name to be delivered from their cruel slavery in Egypt. He heard their cries so He sent Moses down to Egypt to save them. It sounds similar because the circumstances and the salvation[1] that is in view are exactly the same in both cases.

The salvation Paul discussed in his letter to the Romans is only one aspect of the salvation described in the Scriptures. I can liken the salvation that he discussed to the fruit of the Spirit that he listed in Gal. 5:22-23. Just as the term for fruit is singular in Greek, even though it has nine different elements that comprise it, so the term Paul used for salvation is singular, even though there are at least five elements that fully comprise it. But it should be clear even from the one element that Paul discussed in Romans that salvation is distinct from justification and neither issue has anything to do with going to heaven when we die.

---

[1] Cf., Ex. 3:7-9.
[1] Cf., e.g., Ex. 14:13-14.

Chapter 12

The Kingdom: Promised in the OT, Offered in the NT

The Bible is not about heaven and hell; that is, its main message is not about seeking a path to heaven and escaping hell. It is about God's plan for establishing a kingdom upon this earth, a kingdom that displays His glory through a mediatorial rule by humans. Man will rule, but God will get all of the glory. In the world that we live in, such an idea is not only far-fetched, it is impossible to conceive. Man is so self-centered, so power hungry, so corrupt, and deceptively so, that any rule that he might obtain for himself in this life is sure to bring God little glory and himself much more.

…

Jesus is the Messiah, first, foremost, and fundamentally.

…

To isolate Jesus, as though He didn't come to fulfill the promises God gave to the nation of Israel, is to be guilty of overruling God's plan for the earth and mankind. To disconnect Him from the original purposes revealed in the OT is to rewrite the script for human history. Jesus did not come to be the *Savior* of Gentiles; He did not come to create *a new people* forming a new and different "church" as His end game. He is the Messiah of Israel and as such is inextricably bound to that nation, to its divinely granted covenants, and then, by way of extension, to the restoration of all things in order to accomplish His original intent for all human life and for the planet earth as well. Jesus will model the fulfillment of His original commission to man so that all can understand what this earthly life was meant to be.

Jesus came to rule on David's Throne, fulfilling the Davidic Covenant

It is an extraordinary fact that so many pastors, teachers, and leaders not only debate, but finally reject the possibility that Jesus came to rule over an earthly kingdom since it is the express declaration of Scripture. Not only was King David promised *a continuation of his earthly kingdom* in a covenant that God made with him,[1] but the angel who appeared to Mary *explicitly* told her that Jesus was that promised descendant of King David to *continue his earthly kingdom.* Gabriel explained it this way:

> "And behold you will conceive in your womb, and bear a son, and you shall name Him Jesus. He will be great, and will be called the son of the Most High; and **the Lord God will give Him the throne of His father David, and He will reign over the house of Jacob forever; and His kingdom will have no end.**" (Lk. 1:31-33, emphases mine)

It is *David's throne* that will be His throne; it is *David's kingdom* that He will perpetuate; and it is *the house of Jacob* (the father of all twelve tribes of Israel, each tribe coming from one of his sons) over which He will rule as He rules the entire world in righteousness for one thousand years. Neither Israel's kingdom nor the world-wide kingdom is located within the hearts of individual believers. David's throne over united Israel has never

---

[1] 2Sam. 7:12-16.

been located outside of Jerusalem much less in heaven. And His rule is not over the church or over individual believers but over the house of Jacob and over all the other kingdoms on the earth.[1]

So to summarize these observations through a few questions and answers, let me ask: Where did David rule? On the earth. Over whom did David rule? The nation of Israel alone. Where was David's throne? In Jerusalem. What is the meaning of *king* and *kingdom*? The same throughout the Bible: a person ruling over other people, his subjects, upon the earth within a geographical boundary. These are the three elements that all the earthly kingdoms described in the Bible have.

Does anyone have the right to spiritualize these concepts? I think not. Why do some spiritualize these concepts? They do it because they have separated Jesus from the nation that He came to save and from the covenants and promises that He came to fulfill. All these things are spiritualized to "Westernize" the faith, to make it more applicable to the people to whom *we* preachers and *we* teachers are attempting to minister. But by going down this path, a distortion of Biblical concepts has been propagated. And the blame must be laid at *our* doorstep.

Jesus Can't be Ruling Today

There is no rule of Christ Jesus, and there is no kingdom today. Regardless of what some scholars say on this issue, there is no Scriptural support for it, unless of course one reads into the text what it is not saying. Is Jesus upon David's throne today? Is Jesus ruling today? Listen to these passages carefully (all the emphases are mine), and you tell me:

---
[1] Dan. 7:13-14, 26-27.

"So then, when the Lord Jesus had spoken to them, He was received up into heaven, and sat down *at the right hand of God.*" (Mk. 16:19)

"But from now on the Son of Man will be seated *at the right hand of the power of God.*" (Lk. 22:69)

"But being full of the Holy Spirit, he [Stephen] gazed intently into heaven and saw the glory of God, and Jesus *standing at the right hand of God* . . . ." (Acts 7:55, my bracket)

"Who is the one who condemns? Christ Jesus is He who died, yes, rather who was raised, who is *at the right hand of God, who also intercedes for us.*" (Rom. 8:34)

". . . He [God] raised Him from the dead, and *seated Him at His right hand in the heavenly places*, far above all rule and authority and power and dominion, and every name that is named, not only in this age, but also in the one to come. And He put *all things in subjection* under His feet, *and* gave Him as *head over all things to the church*, which is His body, the fullness of Him who fills all in all." (Eph. 1:20-23)

"If then you have been raised up with Christ, keep seeking the things above, where Christ is seated *at the right hand of God.*" (Col. 3:1)

"Now the main point in what has been said is this: we have such *a high priest, who has taken His seat at the right hand of the throne of the Majesty in the heavens* . . ." (Heb. 8:1)

"But He, having offered one sacrifice for sins for all time, sat down *at the right hand of God, waiting* from that time onward *until* His enemies be made a footstool for His feet." (Heb. 10:12-13, quoting Ps. 110:1)

". . . fixing our eyes on Jesus, the author and perfecter of faith, who for the joy set before Him endured the cross, despising the shame, and has sat down *at the right hand of the throne of God.*" (Heb. 12:2)

". . . *who is at the right hand of God*, having gone into heaven, after angels and authorities and powers had been subjected to Him." (1Pet. 3:22)

"He who overcomes, I will grant to him to sit down with Me on My throne, as I also overcame and *sat down with My Father on His throne*." (Rev. 3:21; connect to the scene in heaven described in Rev. 4-5 where only God is sitting on a throne)

Jesus is *never* said to be ruling from the seat that He has taken at the right hand of God the Father. He is not ruling; He is *waiting* . . . for God to set the stage for His coming rule. He is not on His throne reigning over the saints; He is on the Father's throne *interceding* for the saints. He is not the High Prince of Heaven; He is *the High Priest* over the household of God (i.e., over all of His brothers, the *useful* ones and the *useless* ones).

These are the clear, direct affirmations of the Scriptures. Consequently, Jesus can't be ruling today because 1) His throne is in Jerusalem, not in heaven; 2) He is waiting to rule while He is interceding for the saints. To believe otherwise is to be in conflict with the Scriptures. It really is just this simple. We construct different ideas when we are looking through the wrong windowpane at the Scriptures. Our day of accounting for our stewardship of God's Word is coming.[1] We must not take it cavalierly now.

The kingdom of heaven is not in heaven

This should be very plain and self-evident for those who

---

[1] 1Cor. 4:1-2. Cf., 2Tim. 2:15.

have attempted to study this topic apart from the theological biases that are seemingly ubiquitous. Because the kingdom that Jesus offered was the Davidic Kingdom promised to David, it is obvious that the kingdom cannot be in heaven. Matthew would never have begun his gospel with Jesus' lineage if it was ultimately so superfluous to Jesus' reign. No one needs a royal, physical lineage to sit upon a spiritual throne, or to rule over the hearts of people, or to rule from heaven. The kingdom of prophecy is a corporate entity, not an individual entity. Jesus will rule over all nations together, not over each single heart separately.

Furthermore, Daniel assured us that the promised Messianic Kingdom is one that is *under* the heavens not *in* the heavens.[1] The kingdom will be established *on* the earth throughout the land God has promised to give to Abraham and to his descendants.[2] And in the same way, the throne is *in* Jerusalem,[3] not in the heavenly realms. Jesus will not ascend that glorious, Davidic throne *until* He returns to earth.[4]

When Satan in Jesus' third temptation showed Jesus all the kingdoms on earth and offered to give them to Him, why would this have been a temptation or an enticement if He had not come for those very things? Satan knew He had come to reign as king so he offered Him a clear path to reach His goal easily. That Satan had understood Jesus' goal properly is confirmed by the fact that Jesus taught His apostles to pray for the kingdom to come to earth so that God's will would be done in every aspect of life *on the earth* as it is done in every aspect of life in heaven.[5]

---

[1] Dan. 7:27.
[2] Gen. 13:14-17; 15:12-21.
[3] E.g., Ps. 122:1-5; Jer. 3:17; 13:13.
[4] Matt. 25:31.

No one prays to obtain what he already possesses. No one prays for the kingdom to come if it is already here.

The kingdom of heaven is not salvation

The most common mistake is to equate the kingdom of heaven with salvation and both of these with eternal life. So, to be *saved* is to *enter* the kingdom, and to have *eternal life* is to be saved.

...
Eternal life, salvation, and the kingdom are interrelated but not identical.
...

If the kingdom had already begun, even though it was not yet manifested in its fullness as some teach, Jesus could not have been inviting His apostles to enter it because they would have already been in it. Jesus even warned them that they might not even be able to enter the kingdom at all[1] even though they already possessed eternal life.[2] Having and experiencing eternal life are the bases for the future obtainment of Biblical salvation.[3]

In the same way, others have inconsistently suggested that the kingdom is completely spiritual in nature. It is simply Jesus' reign over the heart of the believer. That would mean that the kingdom is present within a believer only to the extent that Jesus is reigning over his heart producing godly character and righteous responses. Every time a believer sins, every time he walks in the flesh, the kingdom disappears. This view is not very convincing because most Christians who are trying to walk

---
[5] Matt. 6:10.
[1] Matt. 5:20; 7:21-27; 18:3.
[2] John 6:47.
[3] John 3:16-18.

with God would readily admit to so many personal issues that Jesus' rule within is almost impossible to identify.

Finally, Daniel's prophecy predicts that the Messiah would be cut off and have nothing.[1] Yet, if, as some suppose, Jesus came to offer people a spiritual salvation, described by the metaphor of a kingdom, then it is impossible to say that He had nothing when He died because many had believed in Him. The very success that John the baptizer and Jesus had in leading people to faith in Jesus proves that the offer of the kingdom is not the same thing as an offer of spiritual salvation. Daniel was speaking about *an earthly reign over the whole nation of Israel*. Jesus certainly didn't have *that* when He was cut off.

The kingdom described in the OT

The kingdom offered by Jesus in the NT is the same kingdom described by God in the OT. It is this kingdom alone that God has promised to set up for Israel and have His Son rule over as He rules over all the other nations as well. What follows are some of the characteristics of the kingdom Jesus was offering so that you can be the judge concerning whether it is here today.

There will be at least one special co-Ruler with the Messiah Himself.[2] If the kingdom is Jesus' internal rule within the heart of man, then King David has already been resurrected and has come into the heart along with Jesus to co-reign there with Him. Yes, that is ridiculous.

This kingdom has a capital city, Jerusalem.[3] The seat of authority is not within the heart, but within Jerusalem, unless, of

---

[1] Dan. 9:26.
[2] Jer. 30:9; Ezek. 34:23-24; 37:24-25; Hos. 3:5.
[3] Isa. 2:2-4

course, God has renamed man's heart Jerusalem. Yes, that too is ridiculous.

This kingdom has a designated place for worship through sacrifice unlike today.[1] If Jesus is ruling today, all believers would be making trips periodically to Jerusalem to worship there. But that could be another part of the *not-yet* kingdom, along with the first two points mentioned above. By the end of this list the reader ought to be getting the idea that the *already-not-yet* concept is almost all *not-yet*! But if it is primarily not-yet here in its fullness, how can we be sure that the little that is supposed to be here is sufficient to identify as part of what should be coming? How can such a view ever be convincing?

This kingdom will not have any stumbling blocks in it at all.[2] This passage requires that when the kingdom is set up, even in its very first moment, there can't be any stumbling blocks within the kingdom. Only a politician, a misguided one at that, would debate the meaning of "in" here. Most believers are by nature stumbling blocks to others.[3]

Every man in this kingdom will be righteous at its beginning.[4] It is past time that we stop this *imputed righteousness* teaching that has been passed on from the Reformation. *The Bible only knows about practical righteous or the lack of it.* This passage is declaring that all of those who are in the kingdom when it begins are practically righteous. All of them! Is that what you see today?

This kingdom begins *when* Jesus ascends David's throne.[5]

---

[1] Ezek. 40-48; Zech. 14:16-18. Today the place of worship doesn't matter (John 4:20-24).
[2] Matt. 13:41-43.
[3] Rom. 14:13, 15, 20.
[4] Matt. 13:43; Isa. 4:2-6; 45:25; 60:21. Cf., Matt. 5:20.

Since Jesus does not sit upon this throne until He returns, He can't rule until He returns. And if He is not ruling from His throne, then the kingdom that is supposed to be present today has no king ruling it. Ahh . . . no wonder there is such chaos in the world today.

All nations will worship Jesus as Israel's Messiah when this kingdom begins.[1] He did not say that *some out of all the nations* will worship Jesus; Jeremiah clearly said that

> "***all the nations*** will be gathered … [and they] shall not walk after the stubbornness of their evil heart." (Jer. 3:17)

Once again the options are either whole sale spiritualization or complete denial since it is impossible to make these statements fit what is observed by objective bystanders today. If the kingdom has already begun, there is so much missing from it that it is unrecognizable.

...

*Only if we disconnect Jesus from His OT Messiahship,
can we have a kingdom today.*

...

Worldwide government will belong to Jesus when the kingdom begins.[2] This is not government over the human heart, but over the nations. This is hardly true today even in a spiritual sense.

Israel will take possession of all of her land at the beginning of the kingdom.[3] Since the rule of Messiah is centered on Israel,

---

[5] Matt. 25:31. Notice the "when" and the "then" in this verse.
[1] Jer. 3:17; Ps. 2:7-8; 22:27.
[2] Isa. 9:7; Rev. 11:15; Dan. 7:27.
[3] Isa. 60:21; Amos 9:15.

if that nation does not have its kingdom, then Jesus, the Messiah of that nation, is not ruling. Simple? Of course it is.

There will be an enormous, personal longevity during this kingdom.[1] And there is some evidence for people living longer, right? But are we able to say that the person who dies at one hundred today is truly unfortunate for having died so early? That will be the age of *the young person* who dies during the kingdom program. Nothing like that is occurring today.

The 12 apostles will rule over the 12 tribes when this kingdom begins.[2] Not only does Jesus have a special co-Ruler in the resurrected King David, all twelve apostles, including Judas, will be raised to rule with Him in the kingdom that He establishes. Again, these twelve thrones are related directly to the twelve tribes of Israel who now have taken possession of all the land given to each tribe. Each apostle is supposed to reign over a separate tribe of Israel during the kingdom. If they are not ruling along with the resurrected King David, then, there is no kingdom today because the kingdom is, first and foremost, about Israel being blessed.

The entire environment will be changed, and the curse upon it will be lifted.[3] The environment will be changed for the better only when Jesus begins to rule in His kingdom. If we really want to save the planet, we ought to understand that its deterioration is caused by a spiritual problem, one requiring belief in Jesus and a walk with Him to fix.

The kingdom can't begin during the Church's presence on

---

[1] Isa. 65:17-23.
[2] Matt. 19:27-28.
[3] Isa. 11:6-9; Amos 9:13, 15. Cf., Hos. 4:1-3 for a contrast.

earth.[1] If the Church is present on planet earth, the kingdom has certainly not begun yet because the Church can't inherit any of it in mortal bodies. I don't see any way around this, do you?

It has a specified duration of 1,000 years.[2] That means that there can be no partial kingdom for 2,000 years and then a fully realized (or actualized) kingdom for 1,000 more years. The duration of this kingdom is for 1,000 years from start to finish. Period. That is the reason it is called a "millennial" kingdom.

The Devil will be bound throughout the duration of this kingdom.[3] With all the spiritual conflicts being experienced by those who have believed in Jesus today, it does not appear that the Devil has been bound. If the Devil has not been bound, the promised kingdom can't be present today.

The last kingdom, that of the Antichrist, must be destroyed *before* Jesus rules.[4] Jesus does not begin to rule until all of His enemies have been defeated. Since that is not true today, there is no kingdom today.

It can't begin before some of the martyred saints from the tribulation are raised.[5] Since some of the martyred saints rule for the entire duration of the kingdom, for all 1,000 years, the kingdom can't begin before their resurrection. Since the Tribulation has not come yet, and since the saints martyred in that period of worldly chaos have not been resurrected, there can't be a kingdom today.

---

[1] 1Cor. 15:50. This is only spoken about believers in the Church, not of believers living after the Church is removed.
[2] Rev. 20:4-7.
[3] Rev. 20:1-3.
[4] Dan. 2:44-45 and its repeat in 7:7-11 is followed by 7:13-14 in which the Messiah then receives His kingdom.
[5] Rev. 20:4.

And finally, the kingdom can't begin until the "times of the Gentiles" have ended.[1] As long as Israel is buffeted by their enemies and Gentiles are in control of the direction that the world is heading, the kingdom has not begun. Israel will have a say in ruling the whole world when the kingdom has really come. As long as the Jews are marginalized, the kingdom has not come.

None of the characteristic elements of the Kingdom listed here are descriptive of an already-not-yet kingdom. All of these elements must be assumed to begin later when Jesus returns to the earth. The *already-not-yet* paradigm must assume that there is a reign of Jesus from heaven and that His heavenly reign is somewhere demanded by the Scriptures. Otherwise, it is obvious that a present day reign of Jesus seems to be quite superfluous. One thing is certain: *a present day reign of Jesus that doesn't fulfill or accomplish any of the elements of the kingdom described in the OT begs the question of its existence or of its usefulness.* Whatever this presumed, present-day reign involves, it has to be minimal at best since there is no evidence of any kingly reign by Jesus today. Everything that is attributed to Jesus' reign today can be found throughout the OT before He ever appeared or ever began this supposed spiritual reign.

I might add one last thought. The kingdom is never described as a gradually forming or a gradually manifested entity. Rather, in both Testaments, the kingdom is set up by a suddenly appearing King who conquers all of His enemies. The kingdom comes upon the earthly scene in cataclysmic fashion, at the end of a spear, so to speak.

---

[1] Lk. 21:24; Rom. 11:25.

And it hardly needs to be noted that the Bible never says that Jesus returns to defeat all the Church's enemies. He isn't the Church's Messiah; He is Israel's. He returns to defeat her enemies and establish her kingdom. If we had not so distorted the message of the Bible by Westernizing it, these truths would be rather self-evident.

Israel's rejection delayed the kingdom

In conformity with the true intent of Daniel's prophecy, Jesus explained that the kingdom was going to be delayed in Lk. 19:11-27.[1] He did not teach that the kingdom was only delayed in its manifestation; He taught that the kingdom had not even been received by the King Himself yet. Again, in conformity with Daniel's prophecy, the kingdom cannot be received until Jesus goes away to obtain it from the Father.[2] And it cannot be established or begun until He returns to earth with the authority to establish it. Presently, He is waiting for the condition of practical holiness to be met by the people of Israel. When it is, He will return, defeat the Antichrist's kingdom, and set up His own millennial throne.[3]

While the kingdom has been delayed, it will certainly come. Jesus made that clear in His post-resurrection teachings to the apostles in Acts chapter one.[4] The task today for the Church is to work for the establishment of the kingdom that is coming. Specifically what task should be the focus of the church? It

---

[1] Dan. 7:13-14; Lk. 19:12. Jesus' parable is based upon the actual, historical events surrounding Archelaus' travel to Roman to receive the kingdom his father, Herod the Great, left when he died. He did not receive it until he went away (to Rome), and it was not established until he returned to rule over it. He is a type of Christ in this scenario.
[2] Lk. 19:12; Dan. 7:13-14.
[3] Lk. 19:12, 15; Dan. 7:18, 21-27.
[4] Acts 1:1-3, 6-7.

ought to share with the whole world, a world by the way filled with prodigals, the grace, love, forgiveness, and power that God offers to connect with the Father in intimate fellowship by the resources that Jesus offers to give freely.

This is the storyline of the Bible and the paradigm it sets before us.

This is the windowpane through which the student of Scripture can properly understand the message in the Bible and the goal of that message.

May God draw us all closer to Himself as we fulfill by the resources Jesus provides the commission He gave at creation.

www.ingramcontent.com/pod-product-compliance
Lightning Source LLC
Chambersburg PA
CBHW062213080426
42734CB00010B/1870